# *the* DIET JOKE

## A Reprogramming Guide for Perpetual Consumers

## *by* LISA PEDACE

## Illustrations by Timothy Warren

BIG SHOT PRESS • SAN DIEGO, CALIFORNIA

D1280379

Printed in the U.S.A.

Copyright © 2010 by Lisa Pedace
ISBN-10  0-9823404-1-9
ISBN-13  978-0-9823404-1-7
Library of Congress Control Number: 2009911960

This book is for informational/entertainment purposes only. It does not take
the place of a visit to your doctor, for which you are probably overdue. The author
and the publisher take no responsibility for any mess you might get yourself into as a
result of reading this book and/or using the information contained herein.

Published by
Big Shot Press
P.O. Box 90932
San Diego, CA 92169

# Acknowledgments

**Thank you** to my excellent editor Jen Howard at The Editorial Department, who, if she got sick of me, was kind enough not to show it. Thank you also, to my outstanding illustrator Timothy Warren, who did get sick of me, and still agreed to illustrate this book.

Thank you to my original fans (and sometimes my only fans): Mom, Dad, Frank, Julie, Mike, and Elizabeth, who I never get sick of.

And thank you to my sugar pie, George, who never gets sick of me. At least, that's what he tells me.

# Contents

# Read this First

**Most diet books** are written by celebrities or doctors, and in extreme cases, by celebrity doctors. I am neither. I'm not a doctor, I'm not a celebrity, and I'm not an expert. In anything.

Why anyone, including me, thinks this qualifies me to write a diet book is beyond comprehension, and yet I have. I'll tell you something else you're not going to like. I don't have a weight problem. Not because I'm one of those naturally thin people who can eat anything they want, but because I'm one of those annoying people who orders dressing on the side.

I do a lot of other annoying things too, like walk every day. Not that walking is so annoying, but I tend to look in other people's windows when I do it and I'm sure the neighbors get tired of it. But I haven't always had these habits. I had to reprogram myself first.

You can reprogram yourself too. Just remember to consult your doctor, or your celebrity doctor if you can get an appointment with him or her, before you do anything. When I wanted to lose some weight, I did not consult anyone and I managed not to kill myself, but I don't recommend that for you because I don't want to get sued.

# PART I

# About Us

I'm on the Dr. Dolittle Diet. I can't eat food. I can only talk to it.

# CHAPTER 1

# Modern Times

## Diets Are a Joke

If you ask me, diets are a joke. Not the funny kind that make us chuckle or laugh, but the mean kind that make us feel worse than we did when the joke started. Why? Because the joke's on us.

Let's start by assuming diets are dysfunctional. What am I saying? I saying that, like families, despite their best intentions, diets tend to screw us up. Sometimes they screw us up so much we no longer know what's normal.

This book is about what's screwed up and what's normal. If you need a hint, what's screwed up is a weight-obsessed culture set smack in the middle of a culture that encourages us to constantly consume everything in sight. What's also screwed up is the message of inadequacy we're fed 24/7 to drive our consumption. Screwed up, too, is the long list of never-ending, quick-fix solutions available for purchase, most of which deliver light results and heavy self-loathing. What's normal is knowing that, as much as we may hate to admit it, if we really want to change something about ourselves, then we have to do the work.

If you picked up this book, I assume you're interested in changing something about you, most likely your pants size. I think I can help. Not because I'm an expert in change or weight loss or nutrition, but because I'm good at wading through crap. In other words, this isn't your mother's diet book. This is a reprogramming guide. In this guide, you'll find information, activities, games, suggestions, humor, and sarcasm—a lot of sarcasm—all designed to help you reprogram yourself, maybe not to be normal (who knows what that is anyway), but to not be so screwed up by the storm of messages we get.

Those messages include:

1. More is better, and
2. We're never enough.

When it comes to food, those messages brainwash us to:

1. Eat constantly, and
2. Rely on "diet" products to lose weight.

But we're getting ahead of ourselves. As with all reprogramming, let's start at the beginning, with the word itself.

## "Diet"

**Diet is a four-letter word and three of the letters spell "die."**

Wow. That's bad from the get-go. No wonder we find the word is so unpleasant. If I ruled the world, I'd throw it out completely. I'd start all over with something positive and affirming, something like *livet*.

"How's your livet?" your doctor could ask and you could smile back and say, "Not bad. My livet's not bad at all." Then he'd pat you on the shoulder and send you home, no charge.

Or your spouse could say, without worry of dishes flying, "Honey, you seem to be spreading. Maybe you should watch your livet." And you could turn to your spouse with big loving eyes and say, "You're right, dear. My livet's too important. I'm going to start paying more attention to my livet right now."

That's what it should have been: *livet*. But instead, it's *diet*. So instead of livet plans and livet recommendations, we're stuck with diet plans and diet recommendations. No wonder people are stuffing themselves to death. The word practically encourages it. It makes you wonder how we ended up with this lemon.

**"Diet" comes from the Greek word "diaita," meaning "a way of life."**

Those doggone Greeks. I can see them now, with their deep tans and curly hair, eating grapes and feta cheese, drinking wine and playing discus on the beach. That's not a bad *diaita* at all. I bet you would love a *diata* like that. Instead you got *diet*, a four-letter word that kicks sand in your face. Talk about a bad translation.

Too bad you can't turn to the back of some flimsy comic book and order some Charles Atlas-like solution, not for frustrated scrawny males, but for frustrated doughy balls like you. Something they could mail to your home in a plain brown wrapper for you to eat or drink or rub on your belly, and then, presto magic, you'd reemerge on the beach a few weeks later, trim, fit, and ready to kick some sand.

Oh, wait. You can. You can order something right now. Diet meals, pills, bars, and creams can be shipped to your door at this very moment. You don't have to be a frustrated doughy ball after all. A new life is just an order form away. Excess fat will melt off your body before your very eyes. You'll be fit and trim in no time. Within weeks, deeply tanned, curly-haired Greeks will invite you to drink wine and play discus on the beach with them. What are you waiting for? Isn't it time you lived better?

That's what the ads say. What nobody tells you, least of all the phone reps and sales folks who just ran your credit card, is that once you stop the meals, pills, bars, and creams, and return to your regular everyday life—the one that got you into this mess in the first place—you will gain back what you have fought so hard to lose, and maybe even then some. And then, not only are you a frustrated overweight doughy ball, you are also a failure.

No wonder you want a cookie. I don't know about you, but I could sure use some inspiration right about now. Lucky I keep some in my pocket for just this kind of thing.

*Our greatest glory is not in never falling,*
*but in getting up every time we do.*

—Confucius

Or as your mother used to say,

*Get up.*

—Your Mother

Get up. Today is a new day—a glorious day—and you only get so many of them, so you better stop taking them for granted.

## The Modern World

If it makes you feel any better, it's not your fault. I mean it's sort of your fault, but I know how hard it is to hear that. What I mean is, it's a modern world and that works against you as much as it works for you.

Consider Oogg, a single caveman. His typical day looks something like this. Wake up. Get club. Leave cave. Look for breakfast. Eat. Look for lunch. Eat. Look for dinner. Eat. Return to cave. Wash club. Make rock bed. Fluff rock pillow. Go to sleep. Repeat.

Oogg doesn't have a weight problem. Oogg is a hunter. Oogg spends most of his day running after food. When Oogg isn't running after food, Oogg is running away from things that see *him* as food. One day Oogg meets Gloga, a pretty young cave woman, and together they have three little cave babies. Gloga leaves the hunting to Oogg and takes upon herself the task of keeping the cave clean and the babies out of the fire.

Gloga doesn't have a weight problem either, because while Oogg is out hunting, Gloga is busy gathering wood for the fire and rocks for her growing dishware collection. Gloga is not sitting at home with a disappearing sleeve of cookies watching game shows.

And what, you wonder, does any of this have to do with you? Absolutely nothing. You're not a cave person. You're a modern person. Your day looks more like this. Wake up. Eat. Drive. Eat. Work. Eat. Shop. Eat. Watch TV. Eat. Sleep. Repeat.

Boy, would Oogg like a day like that. Not because it's so much fun, but at least you don't have dinosaurs chasing you around. That's one of the benefits of being so modern. We don't have to outrun the food chain. Practically everything we eat has been bred and packaged for us. We don't hunt and gather; we drive and take out, or microwave and defrost, or just unwrap and eat.

The problem with this kind of eating is not that it's easy—I'm all for easy—but look up "easy" in the dictionary. It doesn't say a thing about being good for anyone. That's not to say things need to be hard to be good for us. You're not fat because you have a microwave. You're not fat because you have a freezer. You're fat because you're lazy. I don't mean you don't work hard. I'm sure you do. I mean, when it comes to really understanding the relationship between food and your body, you are lazy.

**Lazy means "unwilling to work or use energy," also, "showing or characterized by a lack of effort or care."**

At least that's the definition in the dictionary in my computer. I could get up and check it against the definition in the dictionary in my bookcase, but that's all the way in the other room and I'm too lazy to go get it.

We're all lazy somewhere. There's no fault in that if you can afford it. Oogg would love to be lazy. Oogg would love to relax in his cave, recline in his favorite rock chair and watch cave art all day long, but who would feed the family? Oogg can't just walk to the corner and buy some Dino-Burgers. Even if he could, he'd never make it home. A great big Giganotosaur would get a whiff of the delicious burgers and hunt Oogg down.

Sure, Oogg could throw the Dino-Burgers into the bushes, hoping to divert the Giganotosaur long enough to make it back to the cave, but then he'd have to explain why he came home empty-handed to Gloga, who's got her own hands full with three screaming babies and a clogged rock sink.

## Messages

With this kind of ancestry, is it any wonder humankind is worn out? Who can fault a population for taking the hunt out of the equation if it's in the position to do so? And the modern world is. The food chain has been conquered. The hunter has retired.

**We are the fortunate flabby beneficiaries of progress.**

Everywhere we go, the modern convenience of ready-made food awaits us. Takeout tempts us at every corner. Gas stations have closed the garage and opened a minimart. Supermarkets line their shelves with boxes, bags, and cans of processed ready-to-eat foods. We can hardly step out the door without someone wanting to sell us a pastry.

Even the home is not safe. Little kids selling candy knock on our door. Colorful menus promising quick delivery hang from our doorknob. Third-class advertisements featuring two-for-one burgers and pizza fill up our mailbox. We turn on our television and they hit us again. The grand slam breakfast is back. Value menus seduce us. Singing chocolate candies invite us to play. No wonder we struggle.

### We are bombarded with messages
### to eat every hour of the day.

We must be nuts to think we can lose weight in this environment. That's why, more messages say, if we're trying to lose weight, we better seek help to do it.

Boy, advertisers are clever. They not only tell us what to eat, they solve our every dilemma. No time to cook for your dysfunctional family? Don't worry. Buy this bucket of food and everyone will be normal and happy. Have no buddies to watch the game with? No problem. Buy these chips and beer, and everyone, including attractive members of the opposite sex, will come knocking on your door. Life a little boring? Listen up. Buy these crackers and pop, and toe-tapping music will fill that growing sense of ennui. Getting roly-poly from too many buckets of food, chips, beer, crackers, and pop? We can help. Buy these diet meals, pills, bars, and creams, and watch your fat dissolve in days.

Those people in advertising sure are smart. They know how to fix everything. They must be geniuses. Unfortunately, they must also be liars. Maybe buckets of food and chips and diet pills and everything else they're selling will make us happier, more fulfilled, and more attractive. Or maybe, just maybe, to be happier, more fulfilled, and more attractive, we actually have to do something besides sit on the sofa with a bag of tortilla chips and a can of bean dip.

# How Advertisers Brainwash Us

Standing up to advertisers isn't easy, but we can do it, because despite what we've been brainwashed to believe, we control what we consume. Don't believe me? Let's say it's one o'clock in the morning and for reasons beyond my control, I haven't had a thing to eat since Tuesday. My head's spinning, my stomach's howling, my hands are shaking; I feel weak and dizzy. Thank god there's a 24-hour-anything open. I walk in, and what's this? It's the *Survivor* Minimart. All they offer are boiled cockroaches and pig eyeballs. Am I shopping? No thank you. Am I eating? No way. No matter how hungry I am, trust me, I ain't *that* hungry. Even if they offer me $100,000 and a chance to be on television, the holy grail of modern times, I will pass.

Maybe my example is a little extreme. The point is, when we really want to, we control what we put in our mouth. Boiled cockroaches and pig eyeballs aren't ice cream and pie, and still the point remains: if it's in our mouth, it's usually because we put it there. Everything you ate yesterday you picked up and put in your mouth. Nothing flew in. Nothing magically appeared. Nobody pried open your clenched jaw and shoved in a banana split. You were in charge and on board for most of it. I say "most of it" because of the brainwashing thing.

To understand in part how the brainwashing thing works, let's play a game I call Count the Fat People. The game is to watch some television, but instead of walking out during the commercials, stay in front of the TV, watch the commercials closely, and count the fat people in them.

I played this game as soon as I invented it and watched an hour of *Maury*, starring host Maury Povich. This episode of *Maury*, like many episodes of *Maury*, involved plenty of swearing, some women with big hoo-hoos, and a lot of heckling from the audience.

The first commercial break included:

1. A pretty girl selling herpes medicine.

2. A man in a suit selling get-out-of-debt services.

3. A commercial for a home pregnancy test.

4. A commercial for a vacuum cleaner.

5. A commercial for a nightlight.

From this I deduced the demographic breakdown of people who watch *Maury* include people who are in debt, people who stay at home, and people who have lots of unprotected sex.

**Number of fat people in the commercials:  0.**

The second commercial break of *Maury* included:

1. A commercial for a vaginal anti-itch cream.

2. Another get-out-of-debt commercial.

3. A man in a suit selling aggressive attorney services.

4. A man in a suit selling criminal and DUI defense services.

5. A tease for tomorrow's *Maury* featuring Cheating Lovers.

One starts to wonder if perhaps the people who watch *Maury* wouldn't be better off if they stopped sleeping around so much and got a second job, but that's beside the point.

**Number of fat people in the commercials
(not counting the tease for tomorrow's *Maury*):  0.**

The third commercial break advertised aspirin, which wasn't such a bad idea, so I went to the bathroom to get some. Then I started plucking my eyebrows and missed the rest of the show.

## Commercials Mean Business

Lest you think I just sit around and make up meaningless, meanspirited games, let me explain. I'll do this by example, using a commercial I saw during another show. This particular commercial advertised Hershey's Chocolate Bars and Jet-Puffed Marshmallows, and featured attractive men and women at a beach campfire playing guitars, dancing, and making and eating delicious s'mores.

> **Number of fat people in the commercial: 0.**

I'm sure if I called Hershey's and said something like, "Hey, how come you didn't invite any fat people to your beach party?" they would probably say something like, "Well, we invited them, but they didn't want to come. You know how self-conscious fat people can be."

I say it's more likely Hershey's didn't invite them because Hershey's doesn't want anybody to associate chocolate bars with fat people. Hershey's doesn't want us to connect chocolate with fat. Hershey's wants us to connect chocolate with fun. That's how commercials work.

## Commercials are all about association.

Remember those early erectile dysfunction commercials. The men in the commercials were always attractive, not so old, and in pretty good shape. Why? Because men who have ED don't want to associate themselves with old, unattractive men who can't get it up. And remember the women. The women in the early ED commercials always looked older than the men and were only moderately attractive, as if to say to the man who might buy an ED pill, "We know you wouldn't be having this problem if you were dating Pamela Anderson."

Am I saying you'll never see a fat person in a commercial? No. I've seen them in insurance commercials (as the reason to get insurance) and in prescription drug commercials (as the reason to take prescription drugs) and in diet plan and diet food commercials (as the reason to go on a diet). I just never see them in regular food commercials. Don't you think that's funny? Not funny funny, like I am, but funny odd, like not real.

What does it mean? I'll tell you what I think it means. I think it means the food industry doesn't want us to make any connection between food and fat. If we did that, we might start thinking more about what we buy and how much we eat, and that, my friend, would be bad for business, especially the food and diet business. You may think one has nothing to do with other, but sometimes they meet in dark corners to hold hands and rub noses. Where will they meet next time? How about the company boardroom?

Company boardrooms aren't that romantic unless money turns you on. Take the company boardroom at Nestlé, for example, where brands range from Toll House Cookies to Dreyer's Ice Cream to Jenny Craig Weight Loss. Am I saying Nestlé is the Big Bad Wolf who's trying to fatten us up so we'll, in turn, buy expensive diet products? No. I'm just saying they sometimes meet in the boardroom and shut the door.

What goes on behind closed doors isn't any of our business. Besides, business is business. If Nestlé, just for example, is looking to broaden their customer base and grow their company by buying up another company, the way they did when they bought Jenny Craig for approximately $600 million in 2006, more power to them. I wish I had $600 million. And is there any conflict of interest for a company to sell both chocolate and weight-loss products? No. Nestlé isn't a politician. It's a business. It's all business.

**Selling products is their business.
Taking good care of our body is ours.**

## The Truth

The truth about losing weight is the same as it has always been. You have to burn more calories than you consume. I know it's an easy thing to say, not such an easy thing to do, but you're more talented than you think. If you really committed to it, you would see results. Besides, what are you eating, anyway? You're the king of your body, the king of your mouth, and the king of your food chain. You are not the King of France.

I doubt you're overweight because someone is bringing gourmet food to your table every day. I doubt you live on a five-star luxury yacht where white-hatted chefs prepare silver-plated entrees round the gilded clock. You are overweight, I would guess, because you eat too much, much of it highly processed crap, loaded with fat and sugar, and filled with additives (so it lasts longer) and salt (so you crave more). I would also guess you're overweight because you sit too much. These are the habits of the modern world.

The good news is that reprogramming ourselves is as simple as changing our habits.

*We are what we repeatedly do.*
*Excellence, then, is not an act, but a habit.*

—ARISTOTLE

*So is stuffing our face.*

—LISA PEDACE

## Let's Sum It Up

• Greeks know how to live it up.

• Cavemen did a lot of running.

• The modern world is cranky.

• The point of advertising is to sell you something.

• Mr. Whipple wasn't real.

• You are not the King of France.

• Habits, like hearts, are breakable.

# Reprogramming Activities

## Activity #1—Habit Check

What are some of your modern-day habits? To find out, fill in the following questions.

For breakfast, most mornings, I _____.

For lunch, I frequently _____.

When I come home from work, I usually _____.

My favorite way to wind down is to _____.

When I'm bored, I tend to _____.

My daily exercise routine consists of _____.

My nighttime ritual begins with _____.

I always worry about _____.

A day without _____ is like a day without sunshine.

Now answer this. My three worst habits are:

1. _____

2. _____

3. _____

If you can't come up with anything, ask your partner or anyone else who knows you well. They can probably spit out a dozen. Why is knowing our habits important? Because changing something in our life usually begins with changing some of our habits, and we can't change them until we admit what they are.

## Activity #2—Modern TV Habits

If you're like most Americans, watching plenty of TV is probably one of your modern-day habits. To find out how much of a habit it is, get a piece of paper and write out the following headings at the top of it. Then keep your piece of paper, along with a pen or pencil, near your TV for whole week, and keep track of how often you watch it. Even if you do other things while you watch TV, make a note of every time you turn it on and how long you keep it on.

### TV LOG

| Day | Time On | Time Off | Total Time | Show | Seen It Before |
|-----|---------|----------|------------|------|----------------|
| ___ | ___ | ___ | ___ | ___ | ___ |
| ___ | ___ | ___ | ___ | ___ | ___ |
| ___ | ___ | ___ | ___ | ___ | ___ |
| ___ | ___ | ___ | ___ | ___ | ___ |
| ___ | ___ | ___ | ___ | ___ | ___ |
| ___ | ___ | ___ | ___ | ___ | ___ |
| ___ | ___ | ___ | ___ | ___ | ___ |
| ___ | ___ | ___ | ___ | ___ | ___ |

At the end of the week, add up the total time you spent watching TV. Chew on that for a change.

## Activity #3—Count the Fat People

While you're watching all that TV, why not pay close attention to those commercials and play Count the Fat People.

TV Show _____

Time of Day_____

## COMMERCIAL #1

What were they selling? _____

Who was selling it (not the brand, but the folks in the commercial, i.e. gender, age, implied economic level, implied status level, etc.)?

_____

Number of fat people in the commercial: _____

If there were any fat people, what was their role in the commercial:

_____

## COMMERCIAL #2

What were they selling? _____

Who was selling it? _____

Number of fat people in the commercial: _____

If there were any fat people, what was their role in the commercial:

_____

## COMMERCIAL #3

What were they selling? _____

Who was selling it? _____

Number of fat people in the commercial: _____

If there were any fat people, what was their role in the commercial:

_____


## COMMERCIAL #4

What were they selling? _____

Who was selling it? _____

Number of fat people in the commercial: _____

If there were any fat people, what was their role in the commercial:

_____


## COMMERCIAL #5

What were they selling? _____

Who was selling it? _____

Number of fat people in the commercial: _____

If there were any fat people, what was their role in the commercial:

_____

## Activity #4–
## How Food and Drink Can Solve Your Problems

Now focus just on food and drink commercials. Think about what each commercial implies you'll get if you eat or drink their product. For example, Olive Garden commercials say, "When you're here, you're family." They also show a lot of happy family relationships, whether it's gramps and grandson, or the neat nuclear (not divorced) mom, pop, one son and one daughter out for dinner. What they imply is that happy families eat at Olive Garden, so if you eat at Olive Garden, you'll have a happy family. Is that my opinion? You bet! Three cheers for opinions. Not the loud, obnoxious kind on radio and television, but the small, personal ones we make for ourselves and then offend our friends with.

I'll give you another example. Heineken beer commercials always seem to imply if you drink Heineken, you'll be a little more in the know. Do I drink it? Sure do. Am I in the know? Just ask me!

Oh, and look for fat people too. You won't see many of them selling food (unless they represent "the other brand").

### FOOD OR DRINK ADVERTISEMENT #1

Food or Drink product being advertised: _____

What the commercial implies you'll get from eating or drinking it:

_____

Number of fat people in the commercial: _____

## FOOD OR DRINK ADVERTISEMENT #2

Food or Drink product being advertised: _____

What the commercial implies you'll get from eating or drinking it:

_____

Number of fat people in the commercial: _____

## FOOD OR DRINK ADVERTISEMENT #3

Food or Drink product being advertised: _____

What the commercial implies you'll get from eating or drinking it:

_____

Number of fat people in the commercial: _____

Commercials are an integral part of the brainwashing process. Whatever you ain't got, whether it's love, friends, family, beauty, security, serenity, excitement, or anything else you're lacking, their product will deliver. They promise.

## Activity #5—Let's Set Some Goals

Getting back to you, think about what you'd like to change and fill in the following sentences:

I want to change my _____.

Life is a beautiful thing and when it's not, we can sometimes make it a better thing by making some reasonable changes. We cannot, however, change everything. For example, if I were going to fill in the above sentence, here are some reasonable things I might come up with:

I want to change my weight.

I want to change my lifestyle.

I want to change my spending habits.

Here are some unreasonable things I might come up with:

I want to change my height.

I want to change my leg length.

I want to change my past.

You'll have to decide for yourself if your answers are reasonable. Just a hint: if it requires a time machine, it's probably no good. Also, while modern medicine can do many things, like put water balloons in breasts, they have yet to figure out how to give me longer legs, although they're probably working on it.

Once you've come up with some reasonable possibilities, let's look closer at why you want to change whatever it is you want to change. This is an important step because we want to be sure you're motivated by your own desires, and not someone else's, like advertisers, or your spouse. I'm sure your spouse is a very nice person, but spouses in general are always trying to change something about us that didn't bother them when we were dating. So, using the answers you've already come up with, or even brand-spanking new ones, fill in the following sentence:

I want to change my _____

because I want _____.

Using my same examples from above, I might come up with:

I want to change my weight because I want improve my health.

I want to change my lifestyle because I want to have more energy.

I want to change my spending habits because I want to live more responsibly.

These sentences all represent reasonable goals that are motivated by a reasonable desire of something I want for myself. We're always more likely to have success with something we want for ourselves than we are with goals that are motivated by what other people want from us or we want from other people. For example:

I want to change my weight because I want my mother to stop harping on me.

I want to change my lifestyle because I want my ex to be jealous.

I want to change my spending habits because I want more people to like me.

I understand wanting to make other people do things, like shut up or be jealous or like you more or regret not liking you more. It's fair to want these things. The problem is you can't do anything about them. People are right up there with the weather, traffic, and the economy: we can't control them. Besides that, how can other people possibly know what you expect from them just because you decided not to eat a cupcake?

Finally, let's look at what you want and what you're willing to do about it today.

I want to change my _____ so today I

will _____.


Going back to my earlier responses, I might suggest the following:

I want to change my weight so today I will skip dessert.

I want to change my lifestyle so today I will take a walk.

I want to change my spending habits so today I will brown-bag it.


When you complete the day, check the appropriate box.

☐   I did it!

☐   I started to do it but then _____
                                        (fill in your excuse).

☐   I didn't have time to do it.

☐   I just want to read the book.


Onward, ho!

Mine all goes to my feet.

# CHAPTER 2

# Fat America

## Have You Seen those Americans Lately?

I don't mean to gossip, but people all around the world call us fat. Have you seen those Americans lately, they say? Boy, are they fat—fat and loud. Of course, they've always been a little fat, they say, but now they are *really* fat. They are so fat you hardly notice how loud they are anymore. You can't get past the fat part. And what's with the underwear always showing?

That's what they say. I know it's painful to hear, but you should know how people talk about us behind our backs. Unfortunately, they're right about the fat thing, which brings us to our second game.

Our second game is called Yankee Watch. To play this game, simply go to a public place and look at your fellow Americans. Go to the mall or the park, the game or the pool, any place you like—some place pleasant—park yourself on a bench or a chair, and observe the people around you. How do they look? Pretty average? Overweight? Pillars of health? Is anybody jogging by or is everybody waddling? Anybody eating? Who's eating and what are they eating? Are they eating apples and drinking water? Or are they eating potato chips and drinking soda? Oh, and wear sunglasses. That way people won't see where you're looking. I'd hate for someone to throw their Big Gulp in your face because you won't stop staring at them.

I've played Yankee Watch many times. Call me nosy, but I love to watch other people; it's far more entertaining than TV. One of my observations from playing this game has been that, in general, people don't like to be watched too closely. It makes them nervous. Also, they assume the worst. They assume if you're watching them, you're drawing some kind of unflattering conclusion about them. Often this is true, but I'm not the only one who does it. People draw conclusions about other people all the time, at job interviews, at cocktail parties, in line at the supermarket, in a matter of seconds based on nothing more than appearance.

## Conclusions

What kinds of conclusions do you draw about other people? We'll stick to conclusions about fat people since that's what we're focusing on. I know it's a little awkward, so I'll start.

When I see a fat person I usually conclude that:

1. That person eats too much, or
2. That person sits too much.

Other people might look at fat people and draw different conclusions like:

1. That person is jolly, or
2. That person is not jolly.

I don't know how your weight affects your jollity. If you're a woman, it probably affects it more than if you're a man. That's a general conclusion of mine based on my observation that women are judged by their appearance more than men, and in general women feel bad about this most of the time, at least until they buy some fake boobs. Most people (men and women) who set out to lose weight are generally not jolly because they think they have to embark on something unpleasant, like some horrid family diet cruise, while most people (men and women) who succeed in losing weight are generally jolly, at least temporarily, because they have survived the cruise and can now go home.

That state of jollity can end for two reasons:

1. They gain back the weight they just lost, or
2. They realize that losing weight did not solve their other problems, like credit card debt and ungrateful kids.

Your turn. When you see a fat person, what kinds of conclusions do you make? (Stop and think here.)

You may be missing the point if you conclude that:

1. That person looks fatter than me, or
2. I look pretty good compared to that fat person.

Now imagine a whole county full of fat people. What kinds of conclusions do you make about that? (Stop and think here too.)

Again, you may be missing the point if you conclude that:

1. We all look about the same, or
2. I look better than at least half of them.

There are no right or wrong answers to any of this, so you can come up with anything you like. If you can't come up with something right away, feel free to doodle until you do, but stay at it until you think of something. This whole reprogramming thing isn't going to work if you don't start thinking for yourself. That's why all of us need to get into the habit of making observations and drawing our own conclusions.

**Drawing our own conclusions is like any muscle in our body. If we stop using it, it tends to sag.**

Unfortunately, most Americans are pretty saggy when it comes to drawing their own conclusions. That's because most of us are in the habit of letting others decide what's best for us. The problem with letting others decide what's best for us is that, it's safe to assume, they have their own interests ahead of ours.

When you have completed Yankee Watch, you will probably better understand what most everybody, including you, already knows. More and more Americans are fat and getting fatter every day.

If you counted no fat people at all, you either live on Rodeo Drive or you have become so accustomed to living among fat people you hardly notice them anymore.

By the way, I know what you're thinking. You're thinking I have some strange fixation with counting fat people, but it's not just me. Plenty of businesses, industries, and government agencies are counting too.

## The CDC

Let's start with the government. Starting with government is like jumping into the deep end: not a good idea unless you know how to swim. I don't swim so well, but I can dog paddle my way to the side, and while I may not drown, I will likely swallow lots of chlorine. My pool analogy is probably irrelevant except to illustrate that swallowing chlorine is slightly more attractive to me than doing *anything* with the government. Not because the government is intrinsically bad—although it tends to rot quickly—but because it's so darn deep. Floating around in the deep end is the Centers for Disease Control and Prevention.

The Centers for Disease Control and Prevention, or the CDC, is the federal government agency in charge of counting fat people. Not for fun and games, like we did, but so they can "promote health and quality of life by preventing and controlling disease, injury, and disability." That's from their website. Of course, they don't just count fat people. They count all sorts of sick people. They also conduct research, develop public health policy, promote prevention, and whatever else they can think of to keep

28

the nation's medical bill down.

Established in 1946 as the Communicable Disease Center and head-quartered in Atlanta, Georgia, the CDC initially focused on fighting malaria, and then broadened its scope to include everything from the West Nile virus to the avian flu to bioterrorism and more. I think it's interesting to note that somewhere along the line they changed their name from the Communicable Disease Center to the Centers for Disease Control, but because they were so clever about it, they didn't have to change their stationery.

The CDC has been counting fat people for a while now and here's what they tell us: the situation is not good. Not only is the number of fat people going up, so is the cost of treating them. The government cares about that because, through Medicare and Medicaid, it provides health insurance for one of every four Americans (that's what I meant about keeping the nation's medical bills down). According to the CDC, those extra pounds put us more at risk for things we don't want, like hypertension, Type 2 diabetes, coronary heart disease, high blood cholesterol, stroke, and a lot of other expensive ailments. Does the CDC guarantee that losing weight will prevent us from getting these diseases? No. But they say we can lower our risk by losing weight.

So how many of us are putting ourselves more at risk? Plenty, they say.

**According to the CDC, more than 66% of U.S. adults are overweight or obese.**

Simply defined, "overweight" means weighing too much, which is pretty cut and dry when it comes to things like your luggage allowance, in which case you can pay a little more and no problem.

Overweight is not so cut and dry when we're talking about something as diverse as human beings living in various cultures, responding to ever-changing whims of politics and fashion.

Or is it?

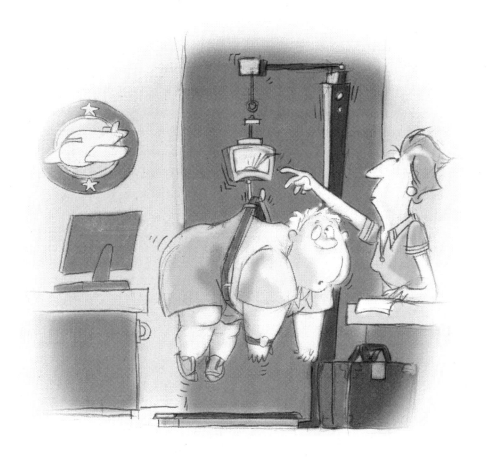

Apparently it is. "Overweight," as far as the government is concerned, is specifically defined as "having a Body Mass Index (BMI) of 25 or more," and "obese" as "having a BMI of 30 or more." According to the CDC, the number of adults aged 20 and older falling into these two categories is at an all-time record high.

And it's not just adults tipping the scales. Kids are fatter than they've ever been too. I guess the days of a gentle nudge from Mom to watch one's waistline are over. Words like tubby, pudgy, and hippy have dropped out of the lexicon. We are now so fat we talk in terms of disease and epidemic. We are now so fat the federal government is involved. That's a sure sign things are bad and about to get worse.

# BMI

For the last few decades, BMI has been the industry standard for determining where we are weight-wise. It's sort of like the old height-weight tables, but better, the industry says, because it takes into consideration other factors like our mother-in-law. It does this with a fairly complicated formula. The formula goes something like this:

> Two cars leave Dallas at 11:00 a.m. One car travels at 75 miles per hour but drives thru McDonald's during the busy lunch hour. The second car travels at 69 miles per hour but stops at Olive Garden and orders the never-ending plate of pasta. Which car will arrive in San Antonio heavier?

The exact formula for BMI looks like this:

$$BMI = (Weight / (Height \times Height)).$$

The formula for stubborn Americans who refuse to convert to the worldwide metric system looks like this:

$$BMI = (Weight\ in\ Pounds / (Height\ in\ inches) \times (Height\ in\ inches)) \times 703.$$

And from where, you ask, did this formula come? BMI is the brainchild of Lambert Adolphe Jacques Quételet, a Belgian overachiever who lived in the 1800s. Quételet was an astronomer, a mathematician, a sociologist, and a statistician. Interestingly, he was not a doctor. You'd think that might be important since we're talking about people's health, but apparently it's not.

Not to make you feel bad, but I've included the annoying chart on the next page. I know at first glance it looks a little like the height and weight tables it supposedly replaced, but it is indeed different. The difference, as far as I can tell, is that now we have license to name-call, but one step at a time. I assume you're already sitting. May I suggest, before beginning, you take a moment and say aloud, "Sticks and stones may break my bones, but names will never hurt me." I hope that helps.

## Body Mass Index Table

| BMI | 19 | 20 | 21 | 22 | 23 | 24 | 25 | 26 | 27 | 28 | 29 | 30 | 31 | 32 | 33 | 34 | 35 | 36 | 37 | 38 | 39 | 40 | 41 | 42 | 43 | 44 | 45 | 46 | 47 | 48 | 49 | 50 | 51 | 52 | 53 | 54 |
|---|---|---|---|---|---|---|---|---|---|---|---|---|---|---|---|---|---|---|---|---|---|---|---|---|---|---|---|---|---|---|---|---|---|---|---|---|
| | Normal | | | | | | Overweight | | | | | Obese | | | | | | | | | | Extreme Obesity | | | | | | | | | | | | | | | |
| Height (inches) | | | | | | | | | | | | Body Weight (pounds) | | | | | | | | | | | | | | | | | | | | | | | | |
| 58 | 91 | 96 | 100 | 105 | 110 | 115 | 119 | 124 | 129 | 134 | 138 | 143 | 148 | 153 | 158 | 162 | 167 | 172 | 177 | 181 | 186 | 191 | 196 | 201 | 205 | 210 | 215 | 220 | 224 | 229 | 234 | 239 | 244 | 248 | 253 | 258 |
| 59 | 94 | 99 | 104 | 109 | 114 | 119 | 124 | 128 | 133 | 138 | 143 | 148 | 153 | 158 | 163 | 168 | 173 | 178 | 183 | 188 | 193 | 198 | 203 | 208 | 212 | 217 | 222 | 227 | 232 | 237 | 242 | 247 | 252 | 257 | 262 | 267 |
| 60 | 97 | 102 | 107 | 112 | 118 | 123 | 128 | 133 | 138 | 143 | 148 | 153 | 158 | 163 | 168 | 174 | 179 | 184 | 189 | 194 | 199 | 204 | 209 | 215 | 220 | 225 | 230 | 235 | 240 | 245 | 250 | 255 | 261 | 266 | 271 | 276 |
| 61 | 100 | 106 | 111 | 116 | 122 | 127 | 132 | 137 | 143 | 148 | 153 | 158 | 164 | 169 | 174 | 180 | 185 | 190 | 195 | 201 | 206 | 211 | 217 | 222 | 227 | 232 | 238 | 243 | 248 | 254 | 259 | 264 | 269 | 275 | 280 | 285 |
| 62 | 104 | 109 | 115 | 120 | 126 | 131 | 136 | 142 | 147 | 153 | 158 | 164 | 169 | 175 | 180 | 186 | 191 | 196 | 202 | 207 | 213 | 218 | 224 | 229 | 235 | 240 | 246 | 251 | 256 | 262 | 267 | 273 | 278 | 284 | 289 | 295 |
| 63 | 107 | 113 | 118 | 124 | 130 | 135 | 141 | 146 | 152 | 158 | 163 | 169 | 175 | 180 | 186 | 191 | 197 | 203 | 208 | 214 | 220 | 225 | 231 | 237 | 242 | 248 | 254 | 259 | 265 | 270 | 278 | 282 | 287 | 293 | 299 | 304 |
| 64 | 110 | 116 | 122 | 128 | 134 | 140 | 145 | 151 | 157 | 163 | 169 | 174 | 180 | 186 | 192 | 197 | 204 | 209 | 215 | 221 | 227 | 232 | 238 | 244 | 250 | 256 | 262 | 267 | 273 | 279 | 285 | 291 | 296 | 302 | 308 | 314 |
| 65 | 114 | 120 | 126 | 132 | 138 | 144 | 150 | 156 | 162 | 168 | 174 | 180 | 186 | 192 | 198 | 204 | 210 | 216 | 222 | 228 | 234 | 240 | 246 | 252 | 258 | 264 | 270 | 276 | 282 | 288 | 294 | 300 | 306 | 312 | 318 | 324 |
| 66 | 118 | 124 | 130 | 136 | 142 | 148 | 155 | 161 | 167 | 173 | 179 | 186 | 192 | 198 | 204 | 210 | 216 | 223 | 229 | 235 | 241 | 247 | 253 | 260 | 266 | 272 | 278 | 284 | 291 | 297 | 303 | 309 | 315 | 322 | 328 | 334 |
| 67 | 121 | 127 | 134 | 140 | 146 | 153 | 159 | 166 | 172 | 178 | 185 | 191 | 198 | 204 | 211 | 217 | 223 | 230 | 236 | 242 | 249 | 255 | 261 | 268 | 274 | 280 | 287 | 293 | 299 | 306 | 312 | 319 | 325 | 331 | 338 | 344 |
| 68 | 125 | 131 | 138 | 144 | 151 | 158 | 164 | 171 | 177 | 184 | 190 | 197 | 203 | 210 | 216 | 223 | 230 | 236 | 243 | 249 | 256 | 262 | 269 | 276 | 282 | 289 | 295 | 302 | 308 | 315 | 322 | 328 | 335 | 341 | 348 | 354 |
| 69 | 128 | 135 | 142 | 149 | 155 | 162 | 169 | 176 | 182 | 189 | 196 | 203 | 209 | 216 | 223 | 230 | 236 | 243 | 250 | 257 | 263 | 270 | 277 | 284 | 291 | 297 | 304 | 311 | 318 | 324 | 331 | 338 | 345 | 351 | 358 | 365 |
| 70 | 132 | 139 | 146 | 153 | 160 | 167 | 174 | 181 | 188 | 195 | 202 | 209 | 216 | 222 | 229 | 236 | 243 | 250 | 257 | 264 | 271 | 278 | 285 | 292 | 299 | 306 | 313 | 320 | 327 | 334 | 341 | 348 | 355 | 362 | 369 | 376 |
| 71 | 136 | 143 | 150 | 157 | 165 | 172 | 179 | 186 | 193 | 200 | 208 | 215 | 222 | 229 | 236 | 243 | 250 | 257 | 265 | 272 | 279 | 286 | 293 | 301 | 308 | 315 | 322 | 329 | 338 | 343 | 351 | 358 | 365 | 372 | 379 | 386 |
| 72 | 140 | 147 | 154 | 162 | 169 | 177 | 184 | 191 | 199 | 206 | 213 | 221 | 228 | 235 | 242 | 250 | 258 | 265 | 272 | 279 | 287 | 294 | 302 | 309 | 316 | 324 | 331 | 338 | 346 | 353 | 361 | 368 | 375 | 383 | 390 | 397 |
| 73 | 144 | 151 | 159 | 166 | 174 | 182 | 189 | 197 | 204 | 212 | 219 | 227 | 235 | 242 | 250 | 257 | 265 | 272 | 280 | 288 | 295 | 302 | 310 | 318 | 325 | 333 | 340 | 348 | 355 | 363 | 371 | 378 | 386 | 393 | 401 | 408 |
| 74 | 148 | 155 | 163 | 171 | 179 | 186 | 194 | 202 | 210 | 218 | 225 | 233 | 241 | 249 | 256 | 264 | 272 | 280 | 287 | 295 | 303 | 311 | 319 | 326 | 334 | 342 | 350 | 358 | 365 | 373 | 381 | 389 | 396 | 404 | 412 | 420 |
| 75 | 152 | 160 | 168 | 176 | 184 | 192 | 200 | 208 | 216 | 224 | 232 | 240 | 248 | 256 | 264 | 272 | 279 | 287 | 295 | 303 | 311 | 319 | 327 | 335 | 343 | 351 | 359 | 367 | 375 | 383 | 391 | 399 | 407 | 415 | 423 | 431 |
| 76 | 156 | 164 | 172 | 180 | 189 | 197 | 205 | 213 | 221 | 230 | 238 | 246 | 254 | 263 | 271 | 279 | 287 | 295 | 304 | 312 | 320 | 328 | 336 | 344 | 353 | 361 | 369 | 377 | 385 | 394 | 402 | 410 | 418 | 426 | 435 | 443 |

Source: Adapted from *Clinical Guidelines on the Identification, Evaluation, and Treatment of Overweight and Obesity in Adults: The Evidence Report.*

32

Now, to the chart. First, find your height in inches. Next, follow across and find your weight. Don't add an inch to your height. Don't subtract three pounds from your weight. Don't round your height up and your weight down. Don't use your height and weight from three years ago. This isn't your driver's license. Finally, look up to find your BMI.

By the way, the opposite chart, for adults 20 years and older, applies to everyone regardless of age or sex. If you're under 20 years of age, your BMI number will be the same, but it's interpreted a little differently to allow for sweet things, like baby fat and puberty.

Your adult BMI will fall into one of the following categories:

| | | |
|---|---|---|
| Underweight | = | less than 18.5 |
| Normal Weight | = | 18.5-24.9 |
| Overweight | = | 25-29.9 |
| Obese | = | 30-39.9 |
| Extreme Obesity | = | 40 and above |

Fill in the following:

My weight: _____

My BMI: _____

My BMI category: _____

The (so-called) Normal (category) Weight range for my height:

_____

I know it's tough to look at all that. That's why a lot of people throw it in the junk drawer next to the sink. And why not? All it leads to is humiliation, and what's the benefit of that? Reality, the government says, reality. Mom may say you need to lose a few pounds, but she'd never call you obese. The government will—to your face. BMI over 25? Overweight! BMI over 30? Obese! BMI over 40? Extremely Obese! That last one is sort of funny since obese already implies extreme, so essentially the government is being redundant, but it wouldn't be the first time.

Critics of BMI say the formula falls short because it doesn't take into consideration other factors like body type and bone density. People who are defending their weight like to include these factors and often do when making statements like, "Sure. I weigh more. I have big bones," or "Sure. I weigh more. I have the body of a walrus." If you're among this group of big-boned flappers, don't worry; another formula exists to upset you. It's called the Waist-to-Hip Ratio formula.

## Waist-to-Hip Ratio

Waist-to-Hip Ratio, or WHR, is calculated not by your height and weight but, not surprisingly, by your waist and hip measurements. To calculate your WHR, simply measure your waist. If you don't have one or can't remember where you put it, measure just above your bellybutton. Then measure your hips at the widest part of your hipbones. Divide the waist measurement by the hip measurement and voilà—you have another thing to feel bad about. Here's the formula to calculate your waist-to-hip ratio. There's no table for this, so you'll have to go it on your own:

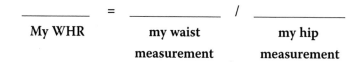

| _____ | = | _____ | / | _____ |
| My WHR | | my waist measurement | | my hip measurement |

Don't be shy. Fill it in. If you have access to a computer, you can find an online calculator to do the computing for you (search "whr calculator").

Sweet spots vary, but in general a ratio less than 0.95 for men, and 0.85 for women is what experts say we're shooting for. A ratio greater than that and we're considered to be "at risk" for heart disease and other problems associated with being overweight.

"At risk" isn't as insulting as "obese," but it hardly makes you sleep better.

## Waist Circumference

There are even easier ways to upset you. Just measure your waist.

**My waist** = _____

For men, you're considered "high risk" if your waist measurement is greater than 40 inches. For women, you're considered "high risk" if your waist measurement is greater than 35 inches. (If you're under 5 feet tall, different rates may apply.)

Waist circumference is important, the government tells us, because we can have a decent BMI and still have too much fat around our waist. Too much fat around our waist, it says, is more dangerous than too much fat around our hips and legs. So, cheer up, ladies and drag queens. That toe-fat might limit the number and type of high-end shoes you can comfortably wear, but according to the government, it's doesn't have the same health implications that abdominal fat does.

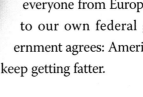

Perhaps you shun formulas and measurements completely. That doesn't get you off the hook. Let me ask you something. Have you ever wondered if you're overweight? Well, as they say in Gucci, if you have to ask, you can't afford it. But enough science for now. The point is, everyone from Europeans to our own federal government agrees: Americans keep getting fatter.

# The Statistics

CDC statistics show that, across the board,
men and women both weigh about 25 pounds more,
on average, than they did some forty years ago.

Statistics also show that the average BMI has increased from 25 to 28. What that tells us is that people who were a little overweight a few decades ago are a little more overweight now. That's no big news. The big news to the folks who pay attention to this stuff is what's happening higher up the scale.

According to the CDC's National Health Center for Statistics, the percentage of overweight but not obese adults rose from 31.5 percent in 1960 to 32.2 percent in 2006. Meanwhile, the number of obese adults rose from 13.4 percent to 35.1 percent. And the number of extremely obese adults rose from practically none to 6.2 percent. So not only are there more fat Americans, there are also more fatter fat Americans. (I learned to describe things that way from the government.)

And there's no sign the trend is receding. Not that the government hasn't tried. Reducing the proportion of adults who are obese has been a national health objective for a decade, along with reducing "the proportion of older adults who have had all their natural teeth extracted," and increasing "the proportion of adults with diabetes who take aspirin at least 15 times per month." Those were just three of the 467 objectives set forth in 2000 as part of Healthy People 2010, a big national prevention agenda that began in 1980 and gets revisited every decade.

I don't know how they did on all their other goals, but America is still fat. Not one state managed to achieve the objective, which was to reduce the number of obese Americans to less than 15%. That's what happens when you have 467 things on your list. You're bound to forget something. Of course, the problem could also be that the government set so many goals, they didn't have any extra time to figure out how to implement them. Rather, they simply encouraged individuals and organizations to select from among the national objectives and build their own agendas. I can't wait to see what they accomplish with Healthy People 2020. I don't mean to say I told you so, but leave it to the government to take things from bad to worse.

Oh, well. At least the media is on it. And how. You can hardly turn on the evening news without hearing about how fat Americans are, usually followed by a commercial for a cholesterol-lowering drug. Fat America may be a costly headache for some, but it's money in the bank for more.

## Businesses and Industries

Businesses and industries, from the health industry to the clothing industry, also keep tabs on fat people, not so they can track and decrease costs, but so they can track and increase profits. Of course, businesses and industries are often too busy counting money to be bothered with counting anything else, so sometimes they pay someone to count for them. This is called market research.

You know what market research is: it's that "product registration" card you mail in to supposedly warranty your new television, or that rebate form you send in to get those few bucks back on your latest purchase, or that online survey you click through to get free shipping the next time you shop. It's even that nice person on the telephone who would like you to answer a few questions before you hang up.

And why not? All market research wants to know is everything: your name, your age, your email, your size, where you shop, if you own, what you drive, how much education you have, your income range, your marital habits, your spending habits, and anything else that will help them understand what you might want to buy next. Then they put all that information together to serve you better. At least, that's one way to look at it.

Take, for example, the plus-size/big-and-tall clothing market. Thanks to Fat America, it's booming—almost fifty percent revenue growth in the last five years. "We're tired of muumuus and poly stretch pants," fat people said, and they backed it up with dollars. Manufacturers will always listen when you back something up with dollars. That's the key to getting their attention. Meanwhile, market research counts how many fat people and how many dollars.

"More than half of the women we're counting are buying plus-size clothes," reports one market research company. "We counted that plus-size women spend more than $900 a year on clothing," reports another. "More than 40% of women wear a size 14 or bigger," reports a third. And the clothing industry, from Tommy Hilfiger to Target, listens.

The food industry listens too, like back in the 1980s when everybody wanted low fat everything. Why low fat? Because somebody (the government, Oprah, whoever) told us we would lose weight if we went low fat. "Low fat," we echoed, "we all want low fat," and just like that, the food industry responded, not with apples and oranges, but with low-fat cookies and crackers. (There's not much profit in unprocessed food.)

The funny thing about that low-fat mania was nobody lost any weight. In fact, most people gained weight. That's what happens when you just replace fat with sugar, which is exactly what the food industry did. Yes, most of the products were lower in fat, but few of them had significantly fewer calories. Those are the kinds of details Americans often skip over when they eat a box of cookies, and eat they did. Obesity soared. People scratched their heads. Maybe this low-fat thing was off track. Maybe fat wasn't so bad. Maybe something else was to blame.

"It's carbs," someone shouted. "Carbs are the devil!" "The devil," we echoed and grabbed our torches. "Sure," the food industry said (they don't care as long as we're buying something) and just like that, hundreds of low-carb products hit the shelves. Carbs were torched. Party conversation dipped to this:

> Stan: Can I offer you a low-carb beer?
>
> Matt: Sure, I hate carbs. I'm glad they're gone.
>
> Stan: They were evil. Want some low-carb chips?

Then you won't believe what happened next. Somebody told us carbs were not the devil and we shouldn't have killed them. Oh well. These kinds of things happen in history. Carbs no longer had to hide in fear. Party conversation bounced back:

> Stan: Want a beer?
>
> Matt: PARR-TEE! Let's meet some chicks!

And now we know the truth. Trans fats are the devil. Before we could blink (or lose our habit for processed snacks) "No Trans Fats" potato chips, cookies, and crackers started appearing everywhere. "Whatever," the food industry says, or rather, "whatever you want." Why?

---

**Because as long as we're consuming, we're always right.**

---

Meanwhile, the collective waistline of America keeps expanding. Hey, at least you don't have to wear a muumuu anymore. And I want you to look nice. We're about to go to one of your favorite places.

## Let's Sum It Up

- Europeans talk about us behind our backs.

- The government is good at making messes.

- Extra baggage is expensive.

- Bulges don't lie.

- Money talks.

- Muumuus are out.

- Omega 3s are in.

# Reprogramming Activities

## Activity #1-Yankee Watch

Next time you're at the ball game or the park or anywhere you like, take a look at the people around you. These are your compatriots. How do we look? Strong and healthy? Thick and padded? If you were an alien visiting your corner of America, what would you report to your leader about our appearance?

## Activity #2—Drawing Conclusions

Nothing smarts like a first impression. Nothing takes less time to make or more time to change. Like it or not, people draw conclusions about us, based on our appearance, in a matter of seconds. Below is a list of words that may or may not describe you. Circle four or five words that do. You can even write in your own words if you like.

| | |
|---|---|
| smart | under exercised |
| stylish | homely |
| attractive | confused |
| successful | competent |
| shifty | lazy |
| dangerous | charming |
| levelheaded | dapper |
| trustworthy | confident |
| poised | handsome |
| ambitious | creative |
| sexy | inert |
| elegant | ambitious |
| neat | unstable |
| unemployable | unwieldy |
| out-of-touch | _____ |
| unapproachable | _____ |
| imaginative | _____ |
| overfed | _____ |

Now look in the mirror and see how you do. Better yet, look at some recent pictures of yourself. (Cameras tend to be more honest than mirrors.) What do you think? Do you present yourself in a way that would lead others to draw these same conclusions or do you need to work on things a bit?

## Activity #3—Making the First Impression You Want to Make

List three things you can do to help you make the right first impression, whatever that is for you. For example, if you would like to be seen as the town floozy (hey, it's right for somebody), then you could: 1. dress scantily, 2. wear thigh-high pleather boots, and 3. apply lots of bright makeup to your face. This look works for rock stars too. This look does not work for women over forty or girls under fourteen, even if your mother or daughter is afraid to tell you so.

Come up with things you can reasonably do now (i.e., update your hairstyle, wear clothes that match, bathe, etc.).

1. _____

2. _____

3. _____

Not sure where to start? Think about someone you met who made a strong first impression on you and see if you can figure why they did. Then use that to guide you. Sometimes it's as simple as being friendly and saying hello to people (no purchase necessary). While you're at it, think about someone you met who didn't make such a strong first impression and see if you can decipher what you based that on (clothing, attitude, smell). Use that to guide you too.

## Activity #4—Being Like Everybody Else

We all like to be a part of the group. Separating ourselves from the group can be isolating, even scary. But sometimes the group is wrong. Take, for example, Nazis.

What do you think about the American group mentality regarding our fat nation? Acceptable, understandable, needs to be changed? What do you think about *your* weight and why? Do you think it's acceptable because most Americans are overweight? Or do you think it's unacceptable, but only because magazines keep telling you to lose weight?

## Activity #5—Market Research

Let's watch some more TV. Pick anything: a ball game, a newscast, a sit-com, and pay attention to the commercials again. Make a list of all the products being advertised.

TV Show _____

Time of Day _____

List of products being advertised:

_____

_____

_____

_____

_____

_____

_____

_____

Now do some market research in reverse. Guess (besides you) who else is watching. How old are they? What are they interested in? What are they worried about?

For example, you see a lot of pharmaceuticals advertised during the evening network news. Why? Because market research shows that older Americans concerned about their health are watching the evening network news. You try.

Market research report for the show you watched:

_____

_____

_____

Try again, but this time, pick a show you wouldn't normally watch.

TV Show _____

Time of Day _____

List of products being advertised:

_____

_____

_____

_____

_____

_____

_____

_____

Market research report for the show you watched:

_____

_____

_____

Making the right choices for each of us depends a lot on our ability to sift through the clutter. Start to see advertisements for what they are—very specific, directed attempts to get your money. Once you do, they'll begin to lose their brainwashing power.

## Activity #6—Product Placement

Guess what? Advertisers aren't just selling to us during the commercials. They're selling to us during the shows too. This is called product placement. Product placement has always been around, but it's getting sneakier. Now products are being written into the script. That's because advertisers know we like to record shows in advance, and fast-forward past the ads. And, according to Nielsen Wire, which show in 2008 had the most product placement? The hit show about weight loss, *The Biggest Loser*, with over 6,000 instances of product placement.

One episode included the following products: 24-Hour Fitness, Star Trac, Brita Water, Cheerios, Fiber One, Jennie-O Turkey, and, ta-dah, The Biggest Loser Fitness Equipment, so we can train just like the folks on TV. Next time you watch your favorite show, see if you notice any products being shoved down your face during it.

# CHAPTER 3

# Land of a Thousand Diets

## The Diet Industry

Of all the businesses and industries that count fat people, none do so with as much love and codependency as the diet industry. The whole of America could slim down and almost everyone, including the clothing and food industries, would survive. XXXL and 32W may become sizes of the past, but people will always need clothes, even if it's unitard space suits. People will always need food too. Sure, the food industry prefers fat people (I assume—they must buy more food), but it can always find another way to package bologna, whether it's Low Fat Bologna-on-a-Stick, Carb Free Bologna Wrap-Ups, or even Omega-3 Rich Bologna and Cheese Space Gelatin Treats.

The diet industry is different.

> **Not only does the diet industry need fat people,**
> **it will shrivel up and melt into the ground like the**
> **Wicked Witch of the West without them.**

The diet industry feeds on fat people, feasts on fat people, can't live without fat people—the way you wished your high school crush couldn't live without you, but, of course, he or she did and married someone else. Who hasn't known that sting of rejection? Who hasn't sat on some quad school bench and watched his or her high school crush walk by hand-in-hand with someone else? For what it's worth, we're better off. Relationships we dream up in our heads never live up to expectations. Still, who forgets the boy or girl who was unaware of our existence?

**The diet industry is not unaware of your existence.
It will never walk by and reject you.**

No, it won't take you to the prom, but it will promise to take you someplace magical. I call this magical place Weight Loss Fantasyland.

## Weight Loss Fantasyland

A regular pilgrimage for many fat Americans, Weight Loss Fantasyland is the kind of place where miracles happen—or, at least, the promise of a miracle, and a quick and easy one at that. And for that promise of a quick and easy miracle, Americans shell out more than $58 billion a year. Visiting is easy too. Usually you don't even have to get off the couch. All you need is a phone, a credit card, high hopes, and a willingness to try something new. Oh, and you have to believe, but that part is easy. If there's anything Americans do well anymore, it's believe, especially in things that sound too good to be true.

Where should you go first? How about Magic World? Magic World is a mysterious place where little magical capsules whisk away all your unwanted fat and excess weight (to dreaded Fat World, no doubt) while you drink from running fountains of chocolate and bathe in warm mineral springs of cream. How does it work? With a big magical whisking motion, the same way doves emerge from black satin hats, the same way people disappear from cages and are replaced by, gasp, growling tigers. Is it safe? Ha ha! I already told you. It's magic! Just close your eyes and believe. Is there any proof it works? Look, do you want magic or don't you? Magic doesn't work when you open your eyes and start asking a lot of questions.

Maybe magic isn't your thing. Maybe you prefer to be pampered. How about a stylish stay in Meal Town? You'll never lift a finger while our highly trained staff of friendly elves appear from behind doors and under doormats at all hours of the day to hand-deliver meals and snacks prepared especially for you. Meal Town is highly endorsed by some of your favorite celebrities. You may even spot one or two of them while you're here. It's always nice to see celebrities. Mostly because it reminds us that they're people too, or we're celebrities also. Something like that, except, of course, it's different. The biggest difference, as far as I can tell, is that they get paid millions of dollars to visit Meal Town and stay in the penthouse while the rest of us pay normal weekly rates to be on the first floor near the service elevator.

In your spare time, don't miss the Expanding Horizons Exhibit Hall. Great, not so great, and overall bad diet ideas from the past, present, and future are on display and available for purchase. Appetite-suppressing toothpaste, fat-burning body spray, cellulite-melting thigh cream, spot-reducing widgets, and more—it's all together here. You can easily spend a whole afternoon and a whole paycheck at the Expanding Horizons Exhibit Hall, and we hope you do.

If you're too weak from dieting to leave your room, don't worry. The Expanding Horizons Network is available 24 hours a day on your television (check your room guide for channel).

Finally, don't miss the historic and impressive Museum of Diets (MOD) where special exhibitions, museum events, and the renowned MOD collection dazzle even the frequent visitor. Recent installations include the provocative "fat Joe on a mound of pink snowballs," and "fat Joe in a pool of melted ice cream."

These are just some of the options. Weight Loss Fantasyland bursts at the seams with options—not following trends, but designing them, continually reinventing itself for you, the insatiable repeat traveler. The big downfall to visiting this popular destination, apart from the cost, is that, like all vacations, it's unsustainable. Sure, you might have some fantastic pictures of where you went and how you looked (like this one here, this is me next to the chocolate fountain, I'm down to a size fourteen in this picture. . .oh, and this one here, next to my favorite elf, I'm down to a size twelve in this. I just look bigger because I'm standing next to an elf), but everything else is fleeting.

## Fantasyland Odds

Just how fleeting the results are is hard to say because Weight Loss Fanta-syland doesn't like to share its secrets (what wizard does?). In "Weight-Loss Advertising: An Analysis of Current Trends," the Federal Trade Commission writes:

> Limited studies paint a grim picture: those who complete weight-loss programs lose approximately 10 percent of their body weight only to regain two-thirds of it back within one year and almost all of it back with five years.

Good thing too. Imagine if we kept the weight off. That'd be bad for business. Weight Loss Fantasyland is hardly built on success. Weight Loss Fantasyland is built on failure! And lots of it. Year after year, it hosts millions of visitors, takes in billions of dollars, and sends home very few winners. Come to think of it, it's not that different from Las Vegas, except that Las Vegas has integrity.

50

That's right! I said it! Las Vegas has integrity. When's the last time Las Vegas promised us anything except to keep its mouth shut? Las Vegas doesn't fib odds. Everybody from the taxi driver to the bellhop to the blackjack dealer tells us the same thing: the house has the advantage, we can't beat the odds, we'll lose in the long run. That's the way Las Vegas works. Somebody has to pay for all that fountain water. It's in the middle of the freaking desert, for god's sake. Besides, they say, with a wink of the eye and a slap on the back, people don't come to Las Vegas to win. People come to Las Vegas to have a good time. If you win, it's a bonus.

Weight Loss Fantasyland should be so forthcoming. Instead, it promises the moon, with words like *easy, effortless, guaranteed,* and *breakthrough.* Red flags, my friend, red flags. The Federal Trade Commission, the Food and Drug Administration, and the National Association of Attorneys General all agree in their brochure called *The Facts About Weight Loss Products and Programs* that words like these are clues: *Clues to Fraud.*

## Clues to Fraud

Let's learn these red-flag words together. I've provided my own definitions based on my own general knowledge and overall common sense, which, on a scale of 1 to 10, rates about a 5.

Easy–not hard
Effortless–minus effort
Guaranteed–for sure
Miraculous–involving miracles
Magical–involving magic
Mysterious–involving mystery
Breakthrough–new discovery
New Discovery–breakthrough
Exotic–sexy something from somewhere else
Secret–I know, but I'm not telling, unless you want to buy it
Exclusive–for me, but not for you, unless you want to buy it
Ancient–very dead

Have you ever seen a slot machine with the word *guaranteed* stamped across it? When you see these words stamped across anything, be wary. Their use is widespread among diet products.

## Repeat Dieters

How many trips have you made to Weight Loss Fantasyland? How many diets have you been on anyway, if you counted them all up? I'll list a few just in case you need to refresh your memory. There is the Abs Diet, the Atkins Diet, the Best Bet Diet, the Body for Life Diet, the Cabbage Soup Diet, the Detox Diet, the Fat Resistance Diet, the Fat Smash Diet, the Fit for Life Diet, the Grapefruit Diet, the High Protein Diet, the Low Protein Diet, the Low Carbohydrate Diet, the Macrobiotic Diet, the Master Cleanse Diet, the Natural Foods Diet, the Organic Foods Diet, the No Grain Diet, the Pritikin Diet, the Scarsdale Diet, the South Beach Diet, the Sugar Busters Diet, the Zone Diets...

Wait! Let's play another game. It's called Guess If They're Real. No, it's not what you think. I'll list some diets and you guess if they're real or not. Circle your answers. The correct answers are at the end of the chapter.

### Guess If They're Real

| | | |
|---|---|---|
| The Hollywood Diet–48-hour miracle juice fast. | Real | Not Real |
| The Moscow Diet–48-hour miracle vodka fast. | Real | Not Real |
| The Blood Type Diet–Blood type determines what you eat. | Real | Not Real |
| The Horoscope Diet–Horoscope determines what you eat. | Real | Not Real |
| The Beverly Hills Diet–First ten days eat only fruit. | Real | Not Real |
| The Beverly Hillbillies Diet–First ten days eat only possum. | Real | Not Real |
| The Lemonade Diet–No food, only lemonade. | Real | Not Real |
| The Lemonhead Diet–No food, only lemonheads. | Real | Not Real |
| Martha's Vineyard Diet–Liquids, colonics, and enemas. | Real | Not Real |

| | | |
|---|---|---|
| Martha Stewart's Diet–Cocktails, canapés, and jail time. | Real | Not Real |
| Morning Banana Diet–Nothing but bananas before 3 p.m. | Real | Not Real |
| Morning Bathroom Diet–Nothing but laxatives before 3 p.m. | Real | Not Real |
| The Negative Calorie Diet–Eat foods that have fewer calories than it takes to digest them, mostly fruits and vegetables. | Real | Not Real |
| The Negative Energy Diet–Eat foods that have no calories and are indigestible, mostly styrofoam and packing peanuts. | Real | Not Real |
| Cavemen Diet–Only eat foods that can be found in the wild. | Real | Not Real |
| Polar Bear Diet–Only eat foods that can be swatted out of the water. | Real | Not Real |

## SUCKER

Did any of these diets sound familiar to you? Did any sound fishy? If they all sound real and plausible, you may have a brainwashing-related dysfunction I just invented called Schizo-Ultra-Crazed-Kooky Eating Regimen disorder, or SUCKER. Not much is known about this disorder since I just invented it, but I assure you it'll be squashed before real medical doctors have even the opportunity to evaluate it. It'll be squashed because dieting industry lobbyists will knock on my door and punch out my lights before proper research can even begin. This is why I will take it upon myself to describe the disorder quickly and look through my peephole before answering the door—a valuable tip in and of itself.

SUCKER disorder is diagnosed when a person displays two or more of the following characteristic symptoms:

- Delusions (Fifty Pounds in Three Days? If I keep that up for a week I'll lose 116.66666 pounds. Then I can have a pizza.)
- More diet books than cookbooks
- Lying scales
- Multiple-sized wardrobes
- Low morale

- Hidden stash of forbidden foods
- Hidden stash of diuretics
- VIP status at the neighborhood donut shop
- Reserved parking at the neighborhood buffet
- Reserved parking at the neighborhood Urgent Care

Treatment for this disorder includes reeducation, regular exercise, positive feedback, and shock therapy. Here comes the shock therapy part:

**You will never keep off the weight you lose when you diet unless you change the way you eat, permanently.**

Wow, that is a shock. You're probably still shaking. If you survive the shock and still want to recover, the prognosis is good.

If you suffer from my newly invented SUCKER disorder, you may have already been diagnosed as a yo-yo dieter. Yo-yo dieters are people who make dieting an extreme sport. They diet dramatically, lose weight quickly, gain it all back fast, and then diet dramatically again. If they're famous, they also pose for magazine covers and do a lot of talk show interviews every step of the way.

Whether or not yo-yo dieting, also called weight cycling, takes a toll on your health isn't exactly clear. The Weight-control Information Network (WIN), a science-based information service of the National Institute of Diabetes and Digestive and Kidney Diseases, says yo-yo dieting *may* be linked to high blood pressure, for example. But then, if you look up "what causes high blood pressure?" the National Heart Lung and Blood Institute admits nobody really knows. It could be a lot of different things, like taxes. And the long-time company line that yo-yo dieting slows up your metabolism hasn't held up either. It turns out the only thing slowing up your metabolism is you. In other words, you can go up and down the diet escalator as many times as you want, and your body, like the trooper it is, will go for the ride. But you would be doing both your body and your psyche a favor if you started taking the stairs.

What is clear is the toll yo-yo dieting takes on your social life. Being on or off a crazy diet all the time makes it awfully hard to calendar parties. I remember Oprah saying, on her show a day or so after she won some special lifetime achievement award, that she didn't even have a glass of champagne to celebrate her award that special night because she was on a diet. She said she had signed some sort of promise of diet commitment to her fitness/diet coach Bob Greene and she was proud to announce that she had honored it.

That was the first time I ever felt sorry for a billionaire. Really, if you aren't going to enjoy a glass of champagne after you've won a lifetime achievement award because you happen to be on a diet that week, then I think you are missing the point. I doubt you will get another special lifetime achievement anything for a while, and certainly not in the next few months. There are only so many of those to go around. You might as well have a glass of champagne to celebrate. Now if Oprah didn't *want* a glass of champagne, that's another story, but she said she did. She said she *wanted* one, but she didn't *have* one because she was on a diet and had signed a piece of paper.

**The moral of the story is always read the fine print.**

I don't want you to sign any piece of paper. If anybody ever calls you up and says, "We're giving you a lifetime achievement award," or even, "We'd like you come over for dinner and give you a pat on the back," please don't say, "Not this week. I'm on a diet." Life is too short to miss out on any occasion where you're the guest of honor. Even if the only time you're the guest of honor is on your birthday, enjoy that moment to the fullest.

Just as you're not overweight because you're the King of France, you are also not overweight because you're the nightly toast of the town. When you're the occasional toast of the town, be sure to show up and revel in the moment. These moments are few and far between. These moments are not to be compared to the evenings you spend alone with your DVD player, a pizza, and a pint of chocolate chip ice cream.

## Diet Defined

If you're a SUCKER who's been brainwashed to yo-yo diet, you probably think of "diet" as something you endure temporarily, like flogging. But the truth is, "diet" just means the food and drink you regularly consume.

Yes, it also means "a restricted intake of food," but that meaning has only gained popularity in recent times because so many people screwed up the first meaning. That is to say, if you were a little better about the food and drink you regularly consume, you wouldn't need to restrict your intake. Yes, I know there are medical and religious reasons to restrict one's diet, but we're talking about you.

What's your diet? Do you know? What do you eat and drink every day? Have you ever thought about it? When people ask me "What's your diet?" I can tell them. I can tell them the kinds of foods I usually eat and the kinds of foods I rarely eat. I can tell them approximately how often I eat certain foods and why. That doesn't make me the Pope. I'm just saying I know what I eat and so should you.

Have you ever asked anybody what he or she eats? Try asking a few people. You'll probably find that people at a healthy weight will answer the question a little more specifically than people at an unhealthy weight. People at an unhealthy weight are more likely to answer generally with words like *anything, everything* and *what's not to eat.*

By the way, asking people what they eat is perfectly acceptable and all together flattering when used in conversations such as, "Gee, you look fantastic. What's your diet?" or "Wow, you haven't aged since high school. What's your diet?" However, when preceded by certain statements, like "You're as big as a horse" or "How do you stay that round?" the question can be considered offensive and is best left to medical doctors who get paid to insult us. In situations like these, the rest of us are better off sticking to less invasive questions like "How much money do you make?" and "Why did you get a divorce?"

## Realistic Goals

Albert Einstein is often credited with saying:

> *Insanity is doing the same thing over and over again and expecting different results.*
> —Maybe Albert Einstein

Or as I like to say,

> *Gambling isn't that much fun when you lose.*
> —Definitely Lisa Pedace

I know you'd like a quick and easy fix. I know you'd like to lose your unwanted extra weight by the weekend. I'd like to finish this book by the weekend. Then we'd both be free for Happy Hour. We could even meet to celebrate. In fact, why don't we do that?

Let's both get on our magical unicorns and ride to TGI Fridays. I'll call the Wizard. Maybe he can join us. We'll all order drinks and while we're waiting for the waitress to return, the Wizard can wave his wand, once over you and once over me, then our drinks will arrive and by the time we finish them and get back on our unicorns, you'll be thinner and I'll be done with this book.

Oh, problem. I just called the Wizard. He's booked. And the unicorns are missing. I guess we're on our own.

So how much time does it take to lose weight? What's your hurry, anyway? Maybe if, as a culture, we didn't demand everything so fast, we wouldn't be in this predicament.

> **Doctors recommend a weight loss of anywhere between half a pound and two pounds a week.**

Things sometimes go a little quicker in the beginning, but expect an average of a pound a week. I know a pound a week isn't very exciting, but it's *safe* and *effective*, popular words in the medical industry, not only because words like *unsafe* and *ineffective* can result in malpractice, but also because if it's done any other way, it doesn't stick.

Don't look so disappointed. Be fair to yourself. You didn't gain that unwanted extra weight overnight and you shouldn't expect to lose it that way either. Besides, how bad is it, really? Let's say you want to lose 25 pounds. If you lose one pound a week, it will take you about six months to achieve your goal. If you want to lose 50 pounds, in six months you're halfway there.

What's wrong with that? You can't get a college degree in six months. You can't pay off your thirty-year mortgage in six months. In fact, get out your calendar and take a look at the last six months. Unless you had some whopper event, i.e., marriage, divorce, birth, death, etc., in which case you shouldn't be trying to lose weight, you should be dealing with the whopper event, then the last six months were probably pretty uneventful. I don't mean that in a bad way, but life is full of chunks of time where things just putter along. So putter along with it. Just putter with less butter.

---

**The goal is not to lose as much weight as you can as fast as you can. The goal is to replace your bad lifestyle habits with better ones—for good.**

---

If that idea, which involves changing what you eat, how much you eat, when you move, and how much you move doesn't interest you, then don't waste your time. Besides the mental wear you put yourself through, who's got that kind of closet space? Fat clothes, thin clothes, really fat clothes, really thin clothes, in-between clothes. Where do you put them all?

Really want to change because this is your body and you want to take better care of it.

## Let's Sum It Up

- People will take your money just because they can.

- There is no Diet Santa Claus.

- Billionaires aren't perfect.

- Fit Elvis was better than Fat Elvis.

- Yo-yos are fun; yo-yo dieting is not.

- The fine print is tiny for a reason.

- The unicorns are always missing.

# Reprogramming Activities

## Activity #1-Celebrity Round Up

Think about some of those celebrities who struggle with their weight publicly. Also consider those who have presented themselves (for a price) as a spokesperson for a specific diet company or plan. How many of them have maintained their weight loss over the long run? (I don't know. I'm just asking.) Why do you think diet companies hire celebrities? Why does what celebrities wear or endorse have so much influence on us regular people? Have you ever bought anything because it was celebrity endorsed? How'd it make you feel? Like a celebrity? Any limos show up at your door? List some products you bought, what celebrity endorsed them, what you expected from the product, and what you got.

| Product | Celebrity endorser | What I expected (fame, more friends, more limos, etc.) | What I got (fame, more friends, just the product, etc.) |
|---------|-------------------|--------------------------------------------------------|--------------------------------------------------------|
| | | | |
| | | | |
| | | | |
| | | | |
| | | | |

## Activity #2—Clues to Fraud Scavenger Hunt

Who doesn't want to be beautiful, thin, rich, and happy? I wouldn't mind being younger either. That's why most of us are suckers for products that promise these things. Whether it's a get-rich-quick scheme, an antiaging potion, or the latest diet pill, chances are some *Clues to Fraud* words are being used to sell it, usually followed by the phrase "Results Not Typical."

Let's do a Scavenger Hunt. See how many of the following words you can find. Look for them in online ads, or in your favorite newspaper or magazine. Listen for them on television and radio too. Next to each word, list the product being advertised.

Ancient _____

Breakthrough _____

Discovery _____

Easy _____

Effortless _____

Exclusive _____

Exotic _____

Magical _____

Miraculous _____

Mysterious _____

New _____

Secret _____

Take another look at the above words. Which words do you fall for? I tend to fall for *guaranteed* and *breakthrough*. Figure out which words you fall for, and then the next time you see them used to advertise some product, try to remember that they're just words, just like *chump, fool,* and *patsy.*

## Activity #3—Your Diet Past

Consider your diet past. What are some of the ways you tried to lose weight and why didn't they work? If they did work initially, what did you do, or not do, that caused you to gain back some of the weight you lost?

| Ways I Have Tried to Lose Weight | Why It Didn't Work or Why It Did Work but Didn't Last |
| --- | --- |
| | |
| | |
| | |
| | |
| | |

Can you learn anything from that list on the right? Do you ever learn from anything you do? (I don't know. I'm just asking.)

## Activity #4—Diet Inquiry

Get nosy. Ask people about their diet and lifestyle. Who knows what you'll find out? Some people might have good habits. Other people might have good surgeons. Write down any useful information you get here.

## Activity #5—Closet Cleanup

Go to your closet and try everything on. Anything that doesn't fit because it's too small, put in one pile. Anything that doesn't fit because it's too big, put in another pile. Anything stained, unflattering, or from the eighties, put in another pile still. Give them all away. Better to have three great-looking items that fit your body well today than 30 not-so-great-looking items that don't. More isn't always more. More often, it's clutter.

## Activity #6—Celebrate Something

I don't know about you, but I will probably never win a Lifetime Achievement Award. That doesn't mean I don't deserve a pat on the back. My guess is that you deserve one too. Write down three things for which you deserve a pat on the back.

1. _____

2. _____

3. _____

Now give yourself one. While you're at it, think about the people in your life who also deserve a pat on the back for something they've done or even something they do every day. Give them a pat on the back too, however you want. Say something nice or do something nice. (Doing something nice doesn't have to involve spending money; you can pick your neighbor's roses.) Everybody needs recognition. Hardly anybody gets it. As a culture, we're so obsessed with celebrities that we overlook the decent, hardworking, friendly people we work and live with every day. Don't overlook the good guys. They may not make the headlines, but they make the world a nicer place. And they show up for jury duty.

*Guess If They're Real Diet Answers:*

The following diets are not real, as in "I made them up" for this particular game. They are: The Moscow Diet, The Horoscope Diet, The Beverly Hillbillies Diet, The Lemonhead Diet, Martha Stewart's Diet, Morning Bathroom Diet, The Negative Energy Diet, and the Polar Bear Diet.

That means all the other diets are real, as in "someone else made them up," and even "you can buy a book by that name," just like you can buy "Real Faux Fur" or "Real Italian Leather–Made in China."

**PART II**

# About Food

Supersize it? I wish I could say that to my husband.

# CHAPTER 4

# It's a Numbers Game, Baby

## A Modern Fable

Let's keep at the reprogramming process and consider what we know about food. One thing we know for sure is there are a lot of lists. There are lists of foods that are good for us and lists of foods that are bad for us. There are lists of foods we should always eat and lists of foods we should never eat. There are green light foods, red light foods, foods that would make your mother blush, and so on.

Lists are great. They are convenient, easy to understand, and something you can post on your refrigerator door, but they can sometimes be misleading. To help illustrate this point, I would like to tell the story of George and the Olive Oil.

Once upon a time there was a man named George. One day George read that olive oil was good for him. This made George very happy, as he loved to eat spaghetti with broccoli and lots of olive oil. Every day George ate spaghetti with broccoli and lots of olive oil and he was always very happy. One day George did not fit into his pants. "It doesn't matter that my pants don't fit," George said, "because I am full of olive oil and olive oil is good for me."

The rest of the story is immaterial. The point is, George doesn't fit into his pants anymore. Yes, olive oil is good for you, but that doesn't mean should you drink it. The moral of the story is a calorie is a calorie is a calorie.

In other words, lists of foods won't help you if you're going to completely ignore calories, for calories are like children: you have to watch them constantly. Even then, they manage to get into everything and ruin the best stuff. They are nothing but little troublemakers.

## A Calorie Primer

How much do we really know about calories? Let's find out. We know the basic concept that calories are like fuel. We know that, like cars, our bodies need fuel to run. However, we also know that if you put too much fuel in your car, it spits out and splashes on your shoes, so calories aren't exactly like fuel, and certainly not as expensive.

**Stomachs are sort of like tanks, but stretchy, and that's a big problem.**

When cars are completely fueled up, they can't hold any more gas. When people are completely fueled up, they can still eat another cookie. Incidentally, when cars are completely fueled up, the weight of the car increases and the gas mileage drops because it's more work to move a heavier load, so next time at the pump, fill'er up halfway. That's a tip I learned from the Automobile Club of Southern California and not bad advice when it comes to eating either.

To really understand calories, we need to understand chemistry, which may explain why so many of us are overweight. For the record, I could barely pass high school science so this should be quick. I was, also for the record, student body president and in my defense, we can't all be good at everything. Let's begin.

Chemistry is that complicated science of the interaction of matter, which we might be inclined to skip altogether were it not for the fact that food is matter and so are we. In fact, long ago we ate food precisely for the chemical interaction that occurred when we ate it.

> **Long ago food was more than just a party for our mouth;
> it was the sustenance of life.**

I'm not kidding. Dictionaries, to this day, define food as any material that is taken in and assimilated by an organism to sustain life and growth. This valuable purpose of food as energy still exists today in many parts of the world where, ironically, there's not enough of it to go around. Perhaps you're aware of this. Perhaps, growing up, you were forced to finish your plate because there were starving children in Africa. A lot of people blame a lifetime of overeating on this childhood family dinner table scenario. Unfortunately, there are still starving children in Africa. Your finishing your plate has not helped the problem at all.

I wish I could report that government and big business are on the problem and it's improving, but I think all they have planned is to pass out more test pharmaceuticals. Human beings will survive without more test pharmaceuticals. They will not survive without enough food, especially the nutritious kind, because food energy is what keeps the body functioning.

> **Just as gas is measured in gallons, the amount
> of energy in food is measured in calories.**

## A Science Experiment

To illustrate this concept, let's conduct a science experiment. Science experiments should always be conducted with proper adult supervision. If you're already an adult, you may conduct this experiment on your own, but as it involves fire, do not do so while under the influence of alcohol or while driving heavy machinery, and certainly not in your pajamas unless they're flame retardant.

I conducted this experiment for the first time in my eighth grade science class and I'd like to take this opportunity to give a shout out to my teacher, but I can't remember his name. To tell the truth, I don't even remember all the steps of the experiment I'm about to suggest, so you may have to fill in some of blanks on your own. Just remember, science sometimes explodes, so don't do anything stupid.

Here's what I remember. We lit a Brazil nut. We stuck a toothpick in it. Then we lit it with a match, and we watched it burn. I conducted the experiment again last night with a macadamia nut, and that works too. I think all nuts are a go. I also tried to light a piece of bread, a pickle, and some butter, but to no avail. The macadamia nut burned a clean, impressive flame for almost a minute before I got bored and blew it out. The bread, the pickle, and the butter just turned black. The fact I was trying to illustrate is that all food has a heat energy value, and that value is measured in calories. The fact I more accurately illustrated is that if you are trying to start a campfire, nuts make better kindling than butter and pickle sandwiches.

You might say science has eluded me, but it wouldn't be the first time. The point is that calories, like fire logs, are stored heat energy waiting to be burned. When we eat food, our bodies burn the food's calories to release energy so our bodies can do things like take out the trash. How this relates to a burning nut, I have no idea, but I ask you: when Moses received the Ten Commandments from the Burning Bush, did he ask how does this relate? In other words, we don't question fire. We get fat when we eat more calories than our body needs and can effectively burn.

Here's another way to think of it. Imagine your body is a big burning fire pit. To keep your fire burning, you have to feed it. If you don't feed it enough, your fire gets smaller. If you don't feed it all, your fire goes out. If you feed it too much, you build a XXXL fire. If you keep feeding your XXXL fire, eventually you have to call for help.

Still confused? Don't worry. I don't take science personally. Here's how the government explains it to children. What you eat and drink is *energy in*. What you burn through regular life and extracurricular activities is *energy out*. If your *energy in* exceeds your *energy out*, your weight goes up. If your *energy out* exceeds your *energy in*, your weight goes down. I personally think igniting nuts makes learning more fun, but that's beside the point.

The point is, some people tell us calories don't matter. Don't worry about calories, they say. Calories are irrelevant, they hoot. Wrong, wrong, wrong! Calories are the key to everything. Believe me, despite everything else you do, when you eat, what kinds of foods you eat, where you eat, all of that is secondary to the fundamental truth about the chemistry of food and your body.

> **If you consume more calories than you burn,**
> **you will gain weight.**
> **If you consume fewer calories than you burn,**
> **you will lose weight.**

Yes, you can make better food choices with sounder nutrition, but until you embrace calories for what they are—little buggers that require your attention—you will never conquer the scale, for calories are like children and fire at the same time. You simply cannot leave them unattended.

Fortunately, while the complicated interaction of food and the body is chemistry, the simple management of calories is basic math. Basic math we can do.

## Calorie Equating

So how many calories do we need? There are a couple of ways to find out. You can pay your doctor or a nutritionist to tell you, or you can look online for a calorie calculator. Most of these calculators are based on the Harris-Benedict Equation, the brainstorm of J. Arthur Harris and Francis G. Benedict, two clever guys who wrote clever papers way back in the early 1900s for the clever Carnegie Institute of Washington. The Harris-Benedict Equation takes into consideration two factors: our basal metabolic rate and our activity level.

Our basal metabolic rate is the total number of calories our bodies need to function without any extras added on, like getting out of bed and toasting a bagel. I'm not saying you have a lot of days quite this lazy, probably just a couple. However many calories it takes to keep you alive while you do essentially nothing, but lie awake in bed, that's your basal metabolic rate. Learn yours now. Like restrooms, there is one for women and one for men.

### WOMEN

655 +  (4.35 X _____ )  +  (4.7 X_____ )

       My Weight in Pounds       My Height in Inches

- (4.7 X_____ )  =  _____

       My Age in Years       My BMR

## MEN

66 + (6.23 X _____ ) + (12.7 X _____ )

My Weight in Pounds          My Height in Inches


- (6.8 X _____ )   =   _____

My Age in Years          My BMR


There you have it. According to Benedict and Harris, that's how many calories you need at your current weight to stay alive on those days when you plan to do nothing, but do it well, as you lie in bed and stare at the ceiling.

But what about those days when you plan to do a little more, like say, go get some burgers, find the remote, and then go back to bed? For those days you need a little more. Why? Because you're taking your car out of the garage, so to speak. How far you take your car determines how many more calories you need. This is often referred to as your Total Daily Energy Expenditure, or TDEE. To find your TDEE, simply multiply your BMR by the appropriate factor from the magic Harris-Benedict Activity Multiplier.

## Harris-Benedict Activity Multiplier

Sedentary          =   BMR X 1.2 (little or no exercise, desk job)

Lightly Active          =   BMR X 1.375 (light exercise/sports)

Moderately Active  =   BMR X 1.55 (moderate exercise/ sports 3-5 days/wk)

Very Active          =   BMR X 1.725 (hard exercise/sports 6-7 days/wk)

Extra Active          =   BMR X 1.9 (hard daily exercise/ sports & physical job or 2x day training, i.e., marathon, race contest etc.)

For the sake of simple math, let's say your BMR is 1,500. If you're sedentary, meaning you get little or no exercise, simply multiply 1500 x 1.2 = 1,800. 1,800 calories is the total number of calories you need to maintain your weight exactly where it is. If you're lightly active, multiply 1500 x 1.375 = 2,062.

Hey, look at that. In this case, the difference between getting no exercise at all and getting moderate exercise a couple times a week is less than 300 calories a day. Interesting. And surprising. I guess one trip to the gym doesn't equal a whole pizza after all. Let's fill in the following:

_____ x _____ = _____

**My BMR**        **My Activity Level**        **My TDEE**

According to the Harris-Benedict Equation, this is how many calories you need to maintain your current weight. Is it exact? Critics say it's not, because it doesn't take into consideration what I like to call the Sprat Factor. The Sprat Factor refers to the Sprats as in:

> Jack Sprat could eat no fat
> His wife could eat no lean
> And so betwixt the two of them
> They licked the platter clean.

According to these critics, if Jack Sprat used the Harris-Benedict Equation to determine his daily caloric requirements, it would probably underestimate the number of calories Jack needs because leaner bodies burn more calories than great big fat ones. Whereas, if Jack's wife used the equation, it would probably overestimate the number of calories she needs. You see, Jack is like a little compact car, burning fuel efficiently, able to park in small places with ease, whereas Jack's wife is a big gas-guzzling SUV, always spilling into the space next to her.

I say the Harris-Benedict Equation isn't exact because it leaves determining one's activity level to oneself, and one has never been very reliable

when it comes to that. Apparently, one likes to think that one gets far more regular and strenuous exercise than one does.

**Getting in and out your car four times a day to get a latte does not make you moderately active. It just makes you moderately irritable.**

I know we live in a society that positively and without apology over-states everything, but try to be honest. You won't make any progress until you are. The truth is most Americans live sedentary lives, and living a sedentary life requires fewer calories.

## Losing Weight

Now that you know about how many calories you need to maintain your current weight, what about how many calories you need to lose weight? Well, a pound of fat equals about 3,500 calories, so if you want to lose a pound of it, you are going to have to use up 3,500 calories of the energy that is already stored up in your body. If you use up 500 calories a day for 7 days, you will lose a pound a week.

> **-500 calories a day x 7 days =**
> **-3,500 calories or minus one pound per week**

There are two ways to use up those already stored calories. One is by consuming fewer calories and the other is burning them off through increased activity. Ideally, you do both. Admittedly, keeping track of how many calories you eat and use is not easy, but ignoring them is worse. Just as cutting back 500 calories a day will result in a pound of weight loss a week; eating an extra 500 calories a day will result in a pound of weight gain a week, as evidenced by all the fat people everywhere.

That's why if you're serious about losing weight, you might want to pay more attention to calories, at least in the beginning.

## Diaries and Food Logs

There are a couple of ways to pay more attention to calories. One is the dreaded food diary. To keep the dreaded food diary, simply record what you ate, when you ate it, where you ate it, why you ate it, how much of it you ate, how you felt when you ate it, how you felt after you ate it, what you were wearing, the weather, the tide, what was on TV, and how many calories you consumed at the time. I can hardly imagine a bigger bore.

Really, what kind of diary is that? Certainly not the kind other people like to read. Imagine the nosy coworker who finds your diary and flips through it only to confirm his or her notion that you're nothing but a pudgy drip.

If you're going to keep an extensive food diary, fine, but at least make it interesting so that when other people read it, they'll think your life is filled with something more than food.

For example:

### A BAD DIARY ENTRY

*9:00 a.m.   Coffee room. Coffee with milk–30 calories. Chocolate donut–300 calories. Ate donut because it was there. Ate standing. Feeling stressed. Didn't really need a donut. Now feeling stressed and guilty.*

## A BETTER DIARY ENTRY

*9:00 a.m.   Coffee room. Coffee with milk–30 calories. Chocolate donut–300 calories. Passed Johnny in the hall. Word in Accounting is that Johnny hooked up Rosie last night after Happy Hour. Rosie is such a hypocrite, all this time pretending to be a lesbian because she thinks it's cool when she's really nothing but a bisexual slut.*

---

**Remember, food is a part of life. It's not a substitute for everything else that gives color to life, like relationships and gossip.**

---

Not quite as awful as the dreaded food diary is the almost-as-dreaded food log. A food log is just that: a log of everything you eat. All that business about how you feel and where you are and what you're doing–the food log doesn't care. Besides, it doesn't matter. You're overweight because you eat too much, relative to how much you move.

I'm sure you're happy as a lark when you eat hot dogs at the ball game. You're probably frustrated as hell when you eat them in traffic. I'm not saying your emotions don't play a role (we'll talk more about them later), but your emotions aren't making you fat, the amount of food you eat is. Your food log will help you understand this.

As in all things, you'll probably find more success if you start small and build from there, so to begin, just write your name on a piece of paper and try to keep that with you all day long. If you manage to keep track of that piece of paper all day long, then the next day, try writing down everything you eat. You may or may not want to write your name at the top of that piece of paper as you have a constitutional right to not incriminate yourself.

Writing down everything you eat isn't that hard, especially if you don't count half the things you put in your mouth, which is common. The unexhausted list of things people don't count includes:

Bites of other people's food

Car snacks

Bread and butter

Chips and salsa

Shared desserts

Liquids

Liquor

Midnight snacks

Food consumed while standing

Food consumed while preparing food

Food on top of other food

Seconds

Things you dip into

Things you spread

Sorry to say, but when it comes to the food log, everything counts, and it's not just what you eat, it's how much too.

That's the hard part, especially in a society that likes to skim over details. Take the muffin, for example. Let's say you have one for breakfast. Unfortunately, writing "one muffin" in your food log leaves a lot of unanswered questions. I don't need to tell you there's no muffin regulation. I'm sure you've noticed for yourself.

For example, a Sara Lee Blueberry Mini Muffin weighs 25.5 grams and has 90 calories. But a Sara Lee Lemon Poppyseed Large Muffin weighs 120 grams and has 460 calories. A milk chocolate chip muffin from Au Bon Pain weighs 156 grams and has 570 calories. A Kirkland blueberry muffin from Costco weighs 162.4 grams and has 612 calories. What is that, anyway? A muffin or breakfast cake for four? Which "one" did you eat? Did you eat 90 calories or 612? There's a difference of over 500 calories.

Lunchtime arrives and you head to McDonald's. Sure, you can write "hamburger, fries, and Coke" in your food log, but what really matters is which hamburger, which fries, and which Coke. Look at the difference between these two meals:

| Hamburger (3.5 oz) | 250 calories | Big Mac (7 oz) | 510 calories |
|---|---|---|---|
| Small fries (2.6 oz) | 250 calories | Large fries (6 oz) | 570 calories |
| Small Coke (16 oz) | 150 calories | Large Coke (32 oz) | 310 calories |
| **Total calories** | **650 calories** | **Total Calories** | **1,390 calories** |

If you ate the Sara Lee Blueberry Mini Muffin for breakfast and the smaller sized meal at McDonald's for lunch, then you're up to 740 calories for the day. If you ate the Kirkland blueberry muffin for breakfast and the larger-sized meal at McDonald's, you're up to 2,002 calories for the day, over 1,200 calories more, and probably all you need for the day. That what I mean when I say it's a numbers game.

By the way, that was the flaw with the movie *Supersize Me*. Sure, Mr. Spurlock got fat when he ate at McDonald's, but he also ate much more than he was accustomed to eating. He ate so much in an early scene that he puked in the parking lot. That wasn't science. That was Mr. Spurlock stuffing his face and then puking in the parking lot. If Mr. Spurlock really wanted to conduct an accurate picture of the effects of eating at McDonald's, he should have eaten only at McDonald's, but maintained his normal caloric intake (the one he had before the film). Would he have gained as much weight as he did? No way. Calories are calories. Yes, there are better nutritional choices than McDonald's out there, but you can just as easily oversize a yogurt fruit smoothie as you can a chocolate milkshake. It all comes down to the numbers.

## Finding the Numbers

So how do you find the numbers? Well, when you can, read the Nutrition Facts label. The Nutrition Facts label comes to us by law, courtesy of the Food and Drug Administration, or the FDA. The FDA is one of the eight U.S. Public Health Agencies within the U.S. Health and Human Services Agency. Here's its mission statement from its website:

> The FDA is responsible for protecting the public health by assuring the safety, efficacy, and security of human and veterinary drugs, biological products, medical devices, our nation's food supply, cosmetics, and products that emit radiation. The FDA is also responsible for advancing the public health by helping to speed innovations that make medicines and foods more effective, safer, and more affordable; and helping the public get the accurate, science-based information they need to use medicines and foods to improve their health.

One might wonder if perhaps it's too much to saddle one agency with everything ranging from cosmetics to veterinary drugs to products that emit radiation to our nation's food supply, but then one wouldn't be thinking like the federal government. One might also wonder if any conflict of interest arises when one agency is simultaneously responsible for "assuring the safety of" and "helping to speed innovations," but then one wouldn't be thinking like the businesses and industries the federal government serves.

**For the government, "protecting the public health" has always been that complicated gray area between how much will we allow and how much money do we want to make.**

Nutrition Facts labels are required by law under the Federal Food Drug and Cosmetic Act to appear on most foods that have been packaged somewhere else and are now in a box or a bag. Nutrition Facts labels are not required at the moment for raw produce (fresh fruits and vegetables) or fish because the government considers these foods "conventional." Why fish is conventional and beef isn't, I don't know, but that's how the government keeps us in line. By confusing us.

There's lots of interesting information on the Nutrition Facts label, but for now let's just consider calories and serving size.

Let's say, for example, you come home from work and go to the fridge. In it you find some macaroni and cheese. Sounds good, you say, and pop it into the microwave. Macaroni & cheese, you write in your food log. Probably two hundred calories, you guesstimate. Is it? I don't know. Check the label.

Let's say this is the label, which I found on the FDA's website. Lucky you, calories are listed right at the top.

# Nutrition Facts

Serving Size 1 cup (228g)
Servings Per Container 2

**Amount Per Serving**

**Calories** 250        Calories from Fat 110

|  | % Daily Value* |
|---|---|
| **Total Fat** 12g | 18% |
| Saturated Fat 3g | 15% |
| *Trans* Fat 3g | |
| **Cholesterol** 30mg | 10% |
| **Sodium** 470mg | 20% |
| **Total Carbohydrate** 31g | 10% |
| Dietary Fiber 0g | 0% |
| Sugars 5g | |
| **Protein** 5g | |
| Vitamin A | 4% |
| Vitamin C | 2% |
| Calcium | 20% |
| Iron | 4% |

**Calories   250**

Not a bad guess, you say,
and pat yourself on the back.
But that's not the whole story.
How much mac & cheese did
you mac? The whole container?
Well, hold on, Charley.
Look at the label again.

**250 is the Amount per Serving.**

How big is a serving?
It's right there at the top too.

**Serving Size 1 cup**

But you ate the whole thing.
How many servings is that?
Back to the label again.

**Serving Per Container 2**

If you ate the whole thing, you ate both servings. That's 250 x 2, which is 500 calories. So, instead of 250 calories, you ate 500 calories. If you need 2,000 calories a day, you just ate a quarter of them.

You'll notice the word "portion" doesn't appear anywhere on the food label. It's mostly semantics but, according to the experts, "portion" now refers to how much we eat, not how much we should have eaten. In other words, the serving size may be one cup, but the "portion" you ate probably wasn't.

**"Portion" used to be almost synonymous with "serving size," until the two no longer resembled one another anymore, and now they hardly speak.**

Sometimes a serving size isn't so easy as half a container. Sometimes it's a lot less, like it is in a big box of cereal, so let's imagine you're having some of that in the morning. Before you just start dumping it from the big box into your big bowl, turn the box around and find the Nutrition Facts label. How much does the label say one serving is? One cup? Half a cup? Is that how much you eat? How should I know? Get out one of your plastic measuring cups and find out. I know it sounds ridiculous to measure your food, but that's what you pay many diet programs to do. Why not save the money and do it yourself?

Do the same thing when you have a glass of orange juice or whatever else you're having for breakfast. Check the serving size on the label and measure out what you're having so you have some idea how many calories you're consuming. Hardly anybody does this.

**What most of us do is let others determine how much we eat and drink.**

We let restaurants decide how much food to put on our plate and we assume it's okay to eat the whole thing. Then we get fat and go on a diet that decides how much to put in our pre-packaged meals. We eat that, lose weight, then we go back to the restaurants and gain it all back.

We buy chips by the bag and assume it's okay to eat the whole bag, except that the bag keeps getting bigger. Everything's bigger, including most of us, which brings up an interesting question.

## Bigger Portion/Bigger American

Which came first: the bigger portion or the bigger American? Like the age-old chicken and egg discussion, do we really have time for this? Aren't we supposed to be measuring cereal? Yes, we are, but it's much more fun to sit around and discuss conspiracy theories of how large corporations make large portions of cheap food to keep large portions of the population fed and placated. How can you revolt if you can't run down the street, let alone carry a musket, without becoming short of breath?

Conspiracy theories can sound ridiculous, but that doesn't mean they're completely without merit, and there's a tour guide at Alcatraz who'll back me up on that, although I don't know his name. (That's the way conspiracy theory backup works; it's never there when you need it.) Alcatraz is the big federal prison in the middle of San Francisco bay that's now closed to prisoners and open to tourists. It's a great place to visit if your travels take you there, which mine did once. While on the tour, our guide directed our attention to the menu chalkboard in the prison cafeteria.

I don't remember what was on the menu, but there was plenty of food. The tour guide told us prison authorities know the best way to keep the inmates under control is to make sure they're well fed. "Who wants to escape on a full stomach?" he said. I agree. I don't even want to wash dishes. Is processed food about social control? Is brainwashing us to eat constantly a simple way of placating the masses? You think the rich didn't learn anything from all those revolutions? People revolt when they're hungry.

Of course, it's economics too. It's simply cheaper to produce large quantities of cheap food to feed large quantities of people. The more cheaply you can feed the masses, the more profits you can put in your pockets. And can you blame the corporations? Are they any different than the rest of us?

The entire modern world, us included, is always trying to do one of two things: make a buck or save a buck, usually both at the same time. That's why we buy the big drink. It's the bargain. We're just being smart shoppers. Corporations are just being smart business companies. It's not their fault we drink the whole thing at once. Corporations aren't selling self-control; they're selling soda. Well, they do sell self-control—if that's what you call diet pills. At least they aren't putting the diet pill formula in the soda and calling it Weight Loss Soda, although I can't say it's not in the works.

## Out to Eat

With the right kind of attention, thanks to labels, measuring cups, and maybe even a food log, you should be able to get a better idea of how much you're eating at home. Everywhere else, it's a different story. That's because restaurants, big and small, all got the big fat exempt from the Nutrition Labeling and Education Act of 1990. Federal law has never required them to provide any kind of nutritional information about the food they serve unless they make some kind of nutritional claim about that item, as in calling it "low fat" or "heart healthy." And even then, the information they provide doesn't have to be precise, it just has to be in the ballpark, so who knows how accurate it really is? Some national restaurant chains have started to post nutritional information online, but because it's not required yet, some post more than others, and some post none at all.

In 2003, the Menu Education and Labeling Act, or MEAL Act, which would have required chain restaurants with at least 20 stores to post calories and nutritional information on menus and menu boards, was introduced to the 108th Congress, but it never became law. It got introduced again in 2006 and again in 2007, and most recently in 2009. Is the fourth time a charm? At the time of this printing, it's not. Some cities, like New York, got tired of waiting and enacted their own mandatory menu labeling rules for large restaurant chains in their city (like New Yorkers need another reason to be pissed off). California was the first state to get on board in 2008, passing a statewide mandatory menu labeling law, which will be fully effective in January 2011. Will that start a trend for the nation? Not if the food and restaurant industries can help it. They don't want us thinking about calories and fat. They want us to spend money. If our arteries take a hit, at least we enjoyed dessert. And if menu labeling does become mandatory, is it beyond business to lie? Hasn't the airline industry taught us anything?

Let's take a short quiz to see how little some eateries care about our health. Believe me, this is just a sampling.

## THE "YOUR HEALTH DOESN'T MATTER TO US" RESTAURANT CALORIE QUIZ

1. A Boneless Buffalo Chicken Salad from Chili's has...
   a. 820 calories     b. 950 calories     c. 1,070 calories

2. A Parmesan Crusted Chicken entrée (no sides) from LongHorn Steakhouse has...
   a. 870 calories     b. 908 calories     c. 1,080 calories

3. A regular Tuna Melt sub sandwich from Quiznos has...
   a. 890 calories     b. 925 calories     c. 1,230 calories

4. A Veggie Quesadilla from Baja Fresh has...
   a. 500 calories     b. 890 calories     c. 1,260 calories

5. A Sirloin Cheese Burger from Jack in the Box has...
   a. 890 calories     b. 920 calories     c. 1,070 calories

6. A Crispy Calamari and Vegetables appetizer from Red Lobster has...
   a. 1,010 calories     b. 1,330 calories     c. 1,520 calories

7. A Chicken and Shrimp Carbonara entrée from Olive Garden has...
   a. 890 calories     b. 1,002 calories     c. 1,440 calories

8. A Carolina Chicken Salad from Ruby Tuesday has...
   a. 500 calories     b. 900 calories     c. 1,007 calories

Answers:

1. C.  A Boneless Buffalo Chicken Salad from Chili's has 1,070 calories.

2. C.  A Parmesan Crusted Chicken dinner from LongHorn Steakhouse has 1,080 calories.

3. C.  A regular Tuna Melt sandwich from Quiznos has 1,230 calories.

4. C.  A Veggie Quesadilla from Baja Fresh has 1,260 calories.

5. C.  A Sirloin Cheese Burger from Jack in the Box has 1,070 calories.

6. C.  A Crispy Calamari and Vegetables appetizer from Red Lobster has 1,520 calories.

7. C.  A Chicken and Shrimp Carbonara entrée from Olive Garden has 1,440 calories.

8. C.  A Carolina Chicken Salad from Ruby Tuesday has 1,007 calories.

Am I saying don't eat these things? No. I'm just saying, if you only need 2,000 calories a day, any one of these items gives you at least half of that, so you might want to skip the fries.

## Calories Count

Get in the habit of paying attention to how much you eat, wherever you are. At home, take the time to check serving size and calories per serving. Measure something out for the fun of it, then throw it on a plate and see what it looks like. At least then, when you're out to eat and they serve you a mound of it, you'll have some idea of what you're looking at. Maybe that means you only eat a quarter of the mound, but what do you think you get when you enroll in all those diet programs? You get small servings. If it helps, use a smaller fork. I know we live in a society that treats food like money: the more you get, the better off you are, but it isn't true.

Lists of food will come and go, but the fundamental truth about food remains the same. If you eat more calories than you need, you will gain weight. If you eat fewer calories than you need, you will lose weight. Forget the trends and get back to the basics.

### Let's Sum It Up

- Calories are not the enemy, but that doesn't mean you can turn your back on them.

- If your gas tank were as stretchy as your stomach, you could hardly afford to drive to work.

- Chemistry is best left to chemists.

- Some people do not have enough to eat. You are not one of them.

- Jack Sprat is in a co-dependent relationship.

- Restaurants don't care about your health.

- Neither does the government.

- Nothing is off-limits if you limit how much you eat.

# Reprogramming Activities

## Activity #1—Home Economics Lab

Let's make some deli-style tuna salad! To begin, get a can of tuna, a jar of mayonnaise, a bowl, a measuring tablespoon, and a mixing spoon. Dump the tuna into the bowl, check the Nutrition Facts label and write down how many calories your can of tuna has. Since you're dumping the whole can, remember to multiply the number of calories per serving times the number of servings per container.

**Calories from tuna** _____

Next, using your measuring tablespoon, add one tablespoon of mayonnaise to the tuna (don't add a heaping tablespoon, it'll screw up our experiment). Check the label on the mayonnaise to see how many calories one tablespoon of mayo has and write it down.

**Calories from 1 tbsp. mayo** _____

Now stir. If your tuna salad needs more mayonnaise, add another tablespoon of mayonnaise (not heaping) to your tuna, and add another tablespoon worth of calories to your total. Add as much mayonnaise as it takes to make it delicious deli-style tuna, but keep track of how many calories you're adding in with each tablespoon.

**Calories from additional tbsp. of mayo** _____

**Total calories for deli-style tuna salad** _____

The point of this activity is to make you realize that, when it comes to calories, *everything* counts. Take, for example, our deli-style tuna salad. It's not just the number of calories a can of tuna has, it's how many calories the mayonnaise has too. This experiment should also make you realize that while tuna can be low in fat and calories, when you order it from the deli case, it ain't necessarily so.

## Activity #2—Home Economics Lab, Part II

Let's try it again with a salad. This time chop up some lettuce and put it on a regular size dinner plate. If you don't want to chop, you can just buy a bag of ready-to-go lettuce. Now add your favorite salad dressing. A serving size of salad dressing is usually 1 ounce (2 tablespoons), so use your measuring tablespoon again and measure out 2 tablespoons of dressing.

Check the label; see how many calories two tablespoons have and write it down here.

**Calories from 2 tbsp. salad dressing _____**

Add as much salad dressing as you like, but keep track of how much you're adding.

**Calories from additional tbsp. of salad dressing _____**

**Total calories for entree-sized salad with dressing _____**

Some salad dressings have 300 calories an ounce, so if you add two ounces (or four tablespoons), that's 600 calories right there. Add another ounce and that's about half your calories for the day. This is important to understand because a lot of us make really decent attempts to eat less by eating different types of salad. The problem is, a salad can be as loaded with fat and calories as french fries, depending on what else is in and on top of it.

## Activity #3—Serving Size Awareness

Let's keep at raising our serving size awareness by trying this. For a day, try to only eat recommended servings sizes. In other words, if you want some cheese and crackers, find out how many crackers make up a serving of crackers, and how much cheese makes up a serving of cheese. Then have that as your snack.

If you want some frozen pizza for dinner, same thing. Check out the serving size and just have that much. Does that mean you can only have one serving of something for the rest of your life? No. It just means you should know what it is.

## Activity #4—Food Log

Now that our awareness of serving size is a little higher, why not give the old food log a try? Write down everything you eat and drink for the whole day. Be as specific as you can. If you have a sandwich, some coleslaw and a cookie, don't just write down "lunch." Include how much of something you eat or drink: 12 ounces of soda is different than 32 ounces of soda. Include all snacks. Include calories too, when you can find them.

If you're out and about and you don't see any labels, ask the friendly people helping you if they have any nutritional information. They may have a brochure in the back behind the mops. If there's no nutritional information available, assume the worst. Then ask yourself how long you're going to keep eating and drinking things without knowing how they affect your efforts to maintain a decent weight.

## FOOD LOG

| What I Ate/Drank | How Much | How Many Calories |
| --- | --- | --- |
| _____ | _____ | _____ |
| _____ | _____ | _____ |
| _____ | _____ | _____ |
| _____ | _____ | _____ |
| _____ | _____ | _____ |
| _____ | _____ | _____ |
| _____ | _____ | _____ |
| _____ | _____ | _____ |
| _____ | _____ | _____ |
| _____ | _____ | _____ |
| _____ | _____ | _____ |
| _____ | _____ | _____ |
| _____ | _____ | _____ |
| _____ | _____ | _____ |
| _____ | _____ | _____ |
| _____ | _____ | _____ |
| _____ | _____ | _____ |
| _____ | _____ | _____ |

Total for the Day _____

At the end of the day, look over your log. What do you think? Good choices? Bad choices? More than you needed? Much more than you needed? Notice any patterns or habits? How many things did you eat without having any idea how many calories were involved? Good idea? Bad idea?

## Activity #5—Online Computing!

Keeping a truly accurate food log can be challenging. Math can be challenging too. If you're not the type to do either well on your own, why not see what tools are out there that can help you. Search online for a calorie calculator and try it out. You'll find everything from free government calculators (no log in required) to whole communities (free and otherwise). Based on the information you put in, they'll tell you how many calories you need to maintain your current weight and how many calories you need to lose weight. Guess what? Both are less than you think.

## Activity #6—Menu Words to Watch Out For

More often than not, we can't get nutritional information when we're out to eat. That doesn't mean we can't make better choices. Below are some commonly used words to describe menu options. Circle those that are better bets for someone who is trying to lose or maintain their weight. The correct answers are at the end of the chapter.

| | | |
|---|---|---|
| Alfredo | Crispy | Platter |
| Au gratin | Crunchy | Poached |
| Baked | Deep-fried | Potpie |
| Battered | Escalloped | Red sauce |
| Béarnaise | Fat free | Roasted |
| Blackened | Fresh | Sautéed |
| Boiled | Fried | Seasoned |
| Bottomless | Giant | Steamed |
| Breaded | Grilled | Stir-fried |
| Broiled | High fiber | Smothered |
| Buttered | Hollandaise | Stroganoff |
| Casserole | Light | Stuffed |
| Cheesy | Loaded | Value |
| Country style | Marinated | Vegetarian |
| Covered | Mega | Vinaigrette |
| Creamed | Multi-grain | White sauce |
| Creamy | Pastry crust | Whole wheat |

## Activity #7—Downsizing Your Appetite

Whether it's soda, frozen yogurt, beer, or whatever else you're ordering, get the small size of everything for a week. For the record, small is just an adjective, defined by Dictionary. com as meaning, "not large as compared with others of the same kind: *a small elephant.*" In other words, a 16-ounce cup of soda is only considered small because you can also buy a jug of it. Yes, I know. Penny-for-penny, you're paying more, but bigger isn't always the best value, all things, including your waistline, considered.

## Activity #8—Consider Hunger

While some of us deal with problems like our expanding pants size and where to hang our new plasma television, other people deal with hunger. In other words, being overweight is a luxury. Instead of using starving children in Africa as a reason to finish your plate, perhaps you could use it as reason to get more involved with the problem of hunger, which affects around 13 percent of the world's population.

Am I saying you should feel guilty about being overweight? Sure. If there's one thing I learned from growing up Catholic, it's that guilt is a powerful motivator. Maybe instead of thinking about what's for dinner, you could think about what you could do to help someone in need. Not sure how to start? Why not host a food drive and donate the collected canned goods to your local food bank?

*Answers to Activity #6*

Better bets are: Baked, Blackened, Boiled, Broiled, Fat free, Fresh, Grilled, High fiber, Light, Multi-grain, Poached, Roasted, Steamed, Stir-fried, Vegetarian, Whole wheat.

Write these words on a Post-It and stick it to your credit card if you need a reminder when you're out to eat.

Just tell him it's someone with a big beef.

## CHAPTER 5

# Food Groups and Other Cliques

## The Food Groups

Getting back to the basics isn't complicated, but it can be confusing. Take the basic four food groups, for example. When I was a kid, the "Basic Four" was a solid four-member ensemble: Dairy; Meat; Fruits and Vegetables; and Grains.

But the "Basic Four" wasn't the original show. Before that it was the "Basic Seven." Before seven, it was twelve, and before twelve, five. Sort of like an ongoing soap opera, characters came and went, plot lines twisted and turned, and ratings went up and down, but the general look of the production remained the same until one day when the big-money producer said, "Time for a new show" and presto magic, the "Basic Four" was cancelled and the "Food Guide Pyramid" was born. Who was this big-money producer? The federal government, of course. Specifically, the U.S. Department of Agriculture, or USDA.

# The USDA

The USDA, or the "people's department" as he proudly called it, was founded by President Abraham Lincoln way back in 1862 to serve what he called "the largest interest of the nation." Indeed, at the time, more than half the U.S. population were farmers.

> **Today, about two percent of the U.S. population are farmers, fewer than the number of people locked up in prison.**

That might lead one to conclude that the USDA didn't do a very good job of protecting the largest interest of the nation, and one might be correct. Still, interests change and the USDA has changed too. Now it hands out food stamps, provides lunches to schoolchildren, takes care of the forest, and promotes and sells U.S. food and agriculture. According to its website, its list of key activities include:

Expanding markets for agricultural products and support international economic development, further developing alternative markets for agricultural products and activities, providing financing needed to help expand job opportunities and improve housing, utilities and infrastructure in rural America, enhancing food safety by taking steps to reduce the prevalence of food-borne hazards from farm to table, improving nutrition and health by providing food assistance and nutrition education and promotion, and managing and protecting America's public and private lands working cooperatively with other levels of government and the private sector.

Wow, that's a lot of food on one plate. At least the USDA hasn't forgotten about the farmer. In fact, "expanding markets for agricultural products" is right there at the top of the list. Sort of sounds like a public relations agency, doesn't it? It makes you wonder if the USDA isn't more interested in promoting food than it is in the quality of the American diet. And why is "improving nutrition and health" so low on the list? These are the kinds of questions that get people audited.

**Just remember this for the rest of your life: food is a business.**

What's that mean for you and me? It means we should always keep in mind motive. Take, for example, Milk and Meat. Way back in 1916 when the USDA guidelines first appeared, Milk and Meat were clumped together as one food group. What did they do? They got their agents on the phone. "You get us each our own group," they both cried, "or we're getting new agents."

And the agents did. Milk and Meat enjoyed separate but equal billing (along with Dairy, Fruits and Vegetables, and Grains) and all the perks that came with it (large dressing rooms, fancy trailers, passes to red carpet events) for decades. Then in 1992, the first pyramid came out. This is what it looked like:

## THE OLD PYRAMID

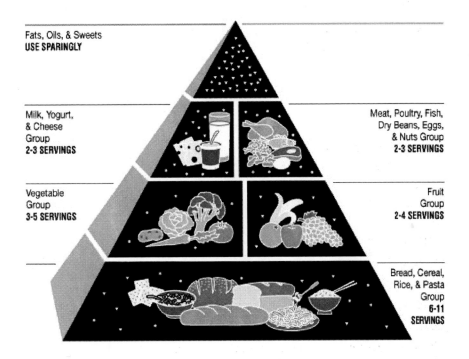

Fats, Oils, & Sweets
**USE SPARINGLY**

Milk, Yogurt,
& Cheese
Group
**2-3 SERVINGS**

Meat, Poultry, Fish,
Dry Beans, Eggs,
& Nuts Group
**2-3 SERVINGS**

Vegetable
Group
**3-5 SERVINGS**

Fruit
Group
**2-4 SERVINGS**

Bread, Cereal,
Rice, & Pasta
Group
**6-11
SERVINGS**

Milk and Meat were indignant. Not only were their names lost on a cluttered marquee, but they both had bad seats up toward the top of the pyramid. What did Milk and Meat do? They got their agents on the phone. "Who do you think you are" they said, "seating us up in the nosebleed seats? America loves Milk and Meat. Milk and Meat built this town. You get Milk and Meat front row seats or we're getting ourselves new agents."

And the agents did. When the USDA released the new MyPyramid in 2005, Milk and Meat weren't any higher or lower than anybody else on the pyramid. In fact, the whole thing was redesigned so that every food group, and now there are six, had some share of front row seats. This is what we call good agenting. The new pyramid looks like this:

### THE NEW PYRAMID

The current food groups are:

> Grains (the Orange slice)
> Vegetables (the Green slice)
> Fruits (the Red Slice)
> Oils & Discretionary Calories (the Yellow slice)
> Milk (the Blue slice)
> Meats & Beans (the Purple slice)

And something else is new: steps have been added to one side of the pyramid to represent Physical Activity. Let's meet the players.

## Grains (the Orange Slice)

Grains are the big stars of the show. Known in the past as *Bread, Flour and Cereals*, Grains are, like all big stars, geniuses at reinvention. According to their press package, Grains are "any food made from wheat, rice, oats, cornmeal, barley or another cereal grain," but the real stars are the good-looking white guys and everybody knows it.

Of course, stars aren't born overnight; they are made, transformed, shoved in your face, and promoted like crazy. A little nip/tuck refinement helps too, which is why most Grains spend a lot of time at The Mills. Bran and germ are okay if you like your stuff heavy, but the masses prefer Grains that are light and fluffy, and nobody ever denies sales.

In recent years, critics have demanded more diversity from Grains, and as result, more Whole Grains are available in the marketplace, especially in the role of Cereals and Breads, but they're often paired up with Sexy White Sugar to make them more appealing to the general population.

| | |
|---|---|
| Former USDA recommended daily allowance: | 6–11 servings |
| Current USDA recommended daily allowance: | |

| | |
|---|---|
| 2,000-calorie diet: | 6 ounces |
| 2,600-calorie diet: | 9 ounces |

What's an ounce? Here are some USDA examples:

> 1 cup of corn flakes
>
> ½ cup of rice
>
> 3 cups of popcorn

You can see the problem with the new pyramid already. An ounce doesn't really equal an ounce. It equals a *government ounce*. What's a government ounce? I could tell you, but then I'd have to kill you. No, just kidding. I didn't know what a government ounce is either, so I emailed the USDA via the "Ask the Expert" link on their Contact Page and asked them. Here was my question:

> **Why is 3 cups of popcorn equal to 1 ounce of grains?**
> **And half a cup of rice is also equal to 1 ounce.**
> **Is it done by weight or calories? Thanks.**

This was their reply:

Hello,

The USDA's MyPyramid Food Guidance System defines Grain Ggroup [their typo, not mine] ounce-equivalents in the same manner as grain servings were defined in the original Food Guide Pyramid (released in 1992). Grain servings in the original Pyramid food patterns were based on two criteria: the diabetic exchange system and serving sizes as commonly eaten. One grain serving was equal to 1 slice of bread, 1 ounce of ready-to-eat cereal, or ½ cup cooked cereal, rice or pasta. MyPyramid uses these same amounts; however, in order to lessen consumer misunderstanding about what constitutes a "serving," recommendations for all food groups were translated to household measures, and the term ounce-equivalent was adopted to define what had been one grain "serving."

The word equivalent is used in a similar way as are diabetic exchange equivalents where the amount for one equivalent varies depending on the type of food. The following count as 1 ounce-equivalent of grain: 1 slice of bread; 1 small muffin (1 oz); 1 cup ready-to-eat cereal flakes; 1 ounce dry pasta or rice; ½ cup cooked rice, pasta, or cooked cereal.

For baked goods, equivalents have been calculated based on the amounts of a product that contains 16 grams of flour. This is because a one-ounce (28-gram) slice of bread contains about 16 grams of flour. This amount of flour was used as a standard in determining the amount that would equal one ounce-equivalent for other baked products only. A standard was needed due to varying moisture contents of baked goods. For example, most bread is purchased in baked, ready-to-eat forms; so, the moisture content is fairly low. Other baked products such as pancakes or crackers have a higher or lower moisture content, so an equivalency based on flour content is used.

The 16 grams of flour standard is not used for products other than baked goods. Hot cereals, pastas, and rice are purchased dry and moisture is added when they are cooked for consumption. Ready-to-eat cereal is purchased as a dry product and is ready for consumption. For these products, a one ounce-equivalent is approximately 28 grams (1 ounce) of the dry product. For products such as rice, pasta, and cooked cereals, approximately one ounce of dry product is equivalent to ½ cup cooked. For popcorn, 1 ounce un-popped equals about 3 cups popped.

Thank You

CNPPsupport
USDA Center for Nutrition Policy and Promotion
3101 Park Center Drive, Suite 1034
Alexandria, VA 22301

Huh? I'm sure glad they wanted to lessen consumer misunderstanding. Imagine if they wanted to compound it.

What they're saying, I think, is that the new USDA recommended daily allowances aren't that different from the old USDA recommended daily allowances, except that they've changed the name, sort of like *Rocky* and *Rocky II*. In other words, a government ounce is equal to a government serving, but it's not always equal to an ounce, which is pretty specific to the rest of the world, especially pot smokers. Oh well. As they say in Hollywood, we can't hold the shoot because the script doesn't make sense. The show must go on!

## Vegetables (the Green Slice)

Next on the bill are Vegetables. Vegetables should be stars, they just aren't. They lack that certain *je ne sais quoi* appeal of refined Grains. If refined Grains succeed because they're blandly simple, Vegetables always seem to come up short, perhaps for seeming too complex and diverse.

Vegetables have always had image problems, and despite recent efforts to heavily promote them, audiences refuse to eat them up. Only Potato, who loves to do B-movies with his slime-ball buddy, Grease, consistently fills seats (and how). A few, like Lettuce, Tomato, and Onion work regularly on Sandwiches and Salads; Peppers and Mushrooms appear occasionally on Pizzas; Carrots have managed to break into the lucrative Kids Afternoon Snack schedule, but most of the others remain misunderstood, difficult to cast, and just not attractive to the general population.

Former USDA recommended daily allowance:   3-5 servings

Current USDA recommended daily allowance:

2,000-calorie diet:   2 ½ cups

2,600-calorie diet:   3 ½ cups

Here are some USDA examples of a cup of vegetables:

1 cup of broccoli

2 cups of romaine lettuce

½ cup of cooked corn

(So not only is an ounce not an ounce, but a cup isn't a cup either. This is what we call, in the biz, "special effects.")

# Fruits (the Red Slice)

Naturally high in sugar content, Fruits are the divas of the food groups. Sometimes exotic, sometimes the girl next door, in their prime, they are all devastatingly seductive, but these exquisite ladies are not without faults. Like all divas, they can be temperamental, impatient, and often unpredictable.

The popular summer concert series, Berries and Melons, is a consistent crowd pleaser that always leaves audiences wanting more, but as any diva knows, familiarity breeds contempt, absence makes the heart grow fonder, and you can't keep ticket prices up if you're always on tour, so the run is short and sweet. In recent decades, even delectable Fruits have seen their demand for live performance decrease as audience preferences switch to more readily available Sweets.

Former USDA recommended daily allowance:    2-4 servings
Current USDA recommended daily allowance:

2,000-calorie diet:    2 cups
2,600-calorie diet:    2 cups

What's a USDA cup? Here are we go again:

½ cup of fruit cocktail
¼ cup of raisins
2 plums

(For the record, Hollywood accounting works the same way too. Nothing adds up, just like on Wall Street. That's what I love about business, industry, and government people. When it comes to numbers, they're all so creative.)

## Milk (the Blue Slice)

Milk and Meat we've already mentioned. The stars of a bygone era, Milk and Meat are long-time industry favorites who refuse to give up audiences they've worked so hard to attract. Milk, like all older leading ladies, has watched her fan base dwindle over the years for a variety of reasons. Mainly, she hasn't aged well. Tabloid reports of rumored abuse haven't helped either.

Rumored or not, unflattering pictures of Milk looking bloated and pasty show up regularly in magazines and on the web. Recurring rehab stints reveal a purported healthier, more organic Milk, but some insiders say, off the record, even the cleaner Milk isn't all that clean. Milk's own popularity may be waning, but she maintains her stronghold, thanks to her talented offspring: Cheese, Yogurt, and Ice Cream. Still, the marquee belongs to Mom. As she gently explained to her girls, it's not a spotlight if four ladies are in it.

Former USDA recommended daily allowance:   2-3 servings

Current USDA recommended daily allowance:

2,000-calorie diet:  3 cups

2,600-calorie diet:  3 cups

What's a cup? Some USDA examples:

1 cup of milk

2 cups of cottage cheese

⅓ cup of shredded cheese

How can 2 cups of cottage cheese equal a cup of milk? I wasn't sure either, so I checked the website (MyPyramid.gov—"Inside the Pyramid"— What counts as 1 cup in the milk group). According to the government, ½ cup of cottage cheese is equal to ¼ cup of milk, so you need four ½ cups of cottage cheese to get 1 cup of milk. That would be well and good except that, according the Nutrition Facts label on a carton of cottage cheese, 1 serving is equal to ½ cup, so you need 4 servings of cottage cheese to get 1 serving of milk. This is what is commonly called a plot hole.

# Meat & Beans (the Purple Slice)

Meat, like all great leading men, has learned to share the spotlight with grace. He's been doing it for decades. Last seen with the ensemble *Poultry, Fish, Beans, Nuts, and Eggs,* Meat has seen his role shift from romantic lead to villain in recent years, but his star power remains undeniable.

His current shared billing with Beans is a head-scratcher, especially considering Poultry's mass market appeal. And when it comes to good press, who gets more of it than Salmon at the moment, so why isn't Fish up in lights anymore? Rumor has it that Beans isn't happy with the recent regrouping because he thinks it soils his healthful image. Still, it's hard to pooh-pooh the exposure.

Is Meat is hoping to attract some of Beans' growing vegetarian audience? Did Poultry and Fish not come to the table with the right bank roll? It's not for us to know. The truth is, deals are made and we're not privy to them until we read about them in the tabloids.

Former USDA recommended daily allowance:     2-3 servings
Current USDA recommended daily allowance:

2,000-calorie diet:     5.5 ounces
2,600-calorie diet:     6.5 ounces

What's an ounce? Examples from the USDA:

1 ounce of chicken

½ ounce of walnuts (about 4 ½ walnuts)

¼ cup cooked black beans

(You know what might make this less confusing? English subtitles.)

## Oils (Part of the Yellow Slice)

Oils used to be a part of the Funny Fat Guys, which in the early years included *Butter, Margarine, Other Fats,* and even *Fat Foods.* Known for their outrageously silly slapstick, the Funny Fat Guys could bust anybody's gut (and they did) until they were blacklisted in the mid-fifties for being unmanageable. The Funny Fat Guys didn't care and began working nonunion to pick up the slack, except for Oils, who started doing summer stock. Starred reviews for Oils soon followed for outstanding performances, including *The Merry Nuts of Windsor* and *The Olive Oil Merchant Of Venice.*

Fats, Oils & Sweets reappeared briefly on the top of the first pyramid, but Oils went solo in 2005 with a new, sophisticated image that is as uppity as ever.

Former USDA recommended daily allowance:   Use sparingly.
Current USDA recommended daily allowance:
2,000-calorie diet:   Aim for 6 teaspoons.
2,600-calorie diet:   Aim for 8 teaspoons.

What's a teaspoon? When it comes to oil, a teaspoon is a teaspoon. However, when it comes to foods that have oil in them, it varies, as in:

2 tablespoons of peanut butter have 4 teaspoons of oil

1 tablespoon of mayonnaise has 2½ teaspoons of oil

1 ounce of dry roasted mixed nuts has 3 teaspoons of oil

(Maybe it's all a dream sequence and when it's over, we find out that the Basic Four Food Groups are still alive!)

## Discretionary Calories (the Other Part of the Yellow Slice)

The other Funny Fat Guys (butter, lard, shortening) ended up with Sweets in the other part of the yellow slice called Discretionary Calories. Why the discretion? Because Fats & Sweets are porn stars. That doesn't mean business isn't booming. Together, this little sliver of so-called discretion accounts for almost half of all food advertising dollars in the U.S. Uptight, tight-lipped government officials may publicly wag a disapproving finger at Fats & Sweets, but that doesn't mean that finger isn't sticky. After all, sugar is a crop too. So is corn (high-fructose corn syrup).

Former USDA recommended daily allowance: Use sparingly

Current USDA recommended daily allowance:

2,000-calorie diet: Limit your extra fat and sugars to 265 calories.

2,600-calorie diet: Limit your extra fat and sugars to 410 calories.

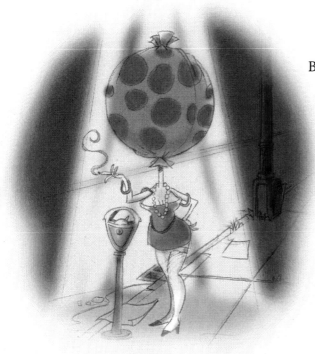

By the way, Fat & Sweets are both G-rated porn stars. That's so advertisers can load Saturday morning programming with them.

And introducing...(music swells)...Physical Activity. Physical activity isn't actually a food group, but try telling the government that. That's like telling them an ounce isn't an ounce.

## Physical Activity & Calorie Recommendations

Physical Activity makes its debut on the MyPyramid as a staircase on the side of it. According to USDA recommendations, all of us should be getting a minimum of 30 minutes of moderate or vigorous activity just about every day to reduce the risk of chronic disease. If we're trying to maintain our weight, or lose weight, or keep off the weight we just lost, we'll probably need more, they tell us, as in 60 to 90 minutes a day.

The USDA makes some basic caloric recommendations too. Here they are for everyone (so you know how much less your spouse should be eating). These recommendations, according to the USDA, are rounded to the nearest 200 calories. Just be sure you round the right way. An extra 200 calories a day can add up to an extra 20 pounds a year.

| Activity Level | | | | |
|---|---|---|---|---|
| Gender | Age (years) | Sedentary | Moderately Active | Active |
| Child | 2-3 | 1,000 | 1,000-1,400 | 1,000-1,400 |
| Female | 4-8 | 1,200 | 1,400-1,600 | 1,400-1,800 |
| | 9-13 | 1,600 | 1,600-2,000 | 1,800-2,200 |
| | 14-18 | 1,800 | 2,000 | 2,400 |
| | 19-30 | 2,000 | 2,000-2,200 | 2,400 |
| | 31-50 | 1,800 | 2,000 | 2,200 |
| | 51+ | 1,600 | 1,800 | 2,000-2,200 |
| Male | 4-8 | 1,400 | 1,400-1,600 | 1,600-2,000 |
| | 9-13 | 1,800 | 1,800-2,200 | 2,000-2,600 |
| | 14-18 | 2,200 | 2,400-2,800 | 2,800-3,200 |
| | 19-30 | 2,400 | 2,600-2,800 | 3,000 |
| | 31-50 | 2,200 | 2,400-2,600 | 2,800-3,000 |
| | 51+ | 2,000 | 2,200-2,400 | 2,400-2,800 |

What do you know? Out of all those nice average normal people, no-body needs 3,500 calories a day. Also interesting, once you pass thirty, your caloric needs go down.

And just so there's no confusion, according to the USDA:

> **Sedentary** is defined as "a lifestyle that includes only the light physical activity associated with typical day-to-day life."
>
> **Moderately active** is defined as "a lifestyle that includes physical activity equivalent to walking about 1.5 to 3 miles per day at 3 to 4 miles per hour, in addition to the light physical activity associated with typical day-to-day life."
>
> **Active** is described as "a lifestyle that includes physical activity equivalent to walking more than 3 miles per day at 3 to 4 miles per hour, in addition to the light physical activity associated with typical day-to-day life."

The USDA also recommends you check your weight regularly and adjust what you're eating if you see any unexpected weight gain or loss. As it says on the website, these recommendations are based on averages, and "the calorie level of the Plan assigned to you probably does not exactly match your calorie needs."

In other words, you're on your own. The USDA has a lot of interests to take care of. You are at the end of a very long line. If you would like to move up the line, I suggest you take out your checkbook.

By the way, if you notice a difference between how many calories the USDA recommends you get and how many calories Mr. Harris and Mr. Benedict recommend you get, it's because the Harris-Benedict Equation calculates how many calories you need to maintain your current weight. The USDA recommendations are based on approximately how many calories the average person needs to maintain a BMI of 21.5 for adult women and 22.5 for adult men, based on a median height.

# A Different Pyramid

The USDA's new pyramid, like the USDA's old pyramid, is (clearly) not without its shortcomings. The good news is that the food pyramid is not like taxes. You can actually ignore the USDA food pyramid and not go to jail. No one will send you threatening letters. No one will attempt to garnish your wages. You won't be penalized at all. You can even design your own pyramid, which is exactly what the smart folks at the Harvard School of Public Health did. Their Healthy Eating Pyramid looks like this:

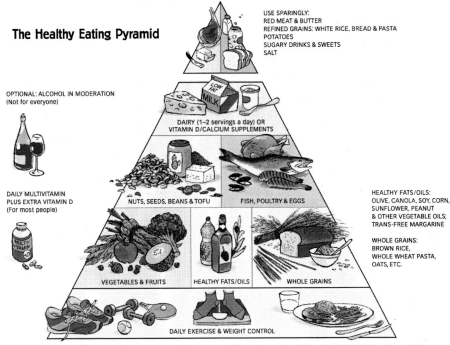

(Copyright © 2008 Harvard University. For more information about The Healthy Eating Pyramid, please see The Nutrition Source, Department of Nutrition, Harvard School of Public Health, http://www.thenutritionsource.org, and *Eat, Drink, and Be Healthy*, by Walter C. Willett, M.D. and Patrick J. Skerrett (2005), Free Press/Simon & Schuster, Inc.)

Look at that. Red meat, butter, white rice, white bread, white pasta, potatoes, and sweets are at the very top of this pyramid. That's right: the whole American diet, right there at the tippy top. Use the American diet sparingly, this pyramid suggests. Down at the base of this pyramid: daily exercise and weight control.

The pyramids don't stop there. The Mayo Clinic made one. The Old-ways Preservation Trust made four: the Mediterranean Diet Pyramid, the Asian Diet Pyramid, the Latin American Diet Pyramid, and the Vegetarian Diet Pyramid, which just goes to show, there's no one pyramid that is right for everyone.

And who says it has to be a pyramid? Nobody.

**The truth is, there are very few absolutes out there.**

## Your Own Food House

If pyramids are optional, and they are, why not design your own food house? Lots of governments have done it using whatever works for them. Canada has a four-banded rainbow. England has a plate. Italy has a leaning tower of food. (Okay, that one I made up.) The point is, you're free to design any kind of food structure you want. Of course, you're going to eat there, so make it nice. Don't design a sugary gingerbread house or a greasy roadside diner.

Not sure what to put in your food house? According to the World Health Organization (a United Nations agency), basic diet recommendations for all populations include:

- Increasing the consumption of fruits, vegetables, legumes (beans), whole grains, and nuts

- Limiting sugars

- Limiting salt

- Limiting total fats and shifting fat consumption from saturated fats to unsaturated fats

- Eliminating trans fats

In other words, don't fill up your house with junk. I know a nice food house filled with fruits, vegetables, whole grains, and nuts is a far cry from the 24-hour roach coach most of us live in now, but if we want to reprogram ourselves, it's time to clean up the digs. The USDA, like the government as a whole, like our parents sometimes, wants what's best for us, according to its agenda, not ours. Isn't it time we start thinking for ourselves?

## Let's Sum It Up

- It's good to have friends in high places.

- It's not just Italians who muscle people into things.

- The government should buy a better set of measuring cups.

- Having a valued opinion is important. Having a valued agent is better.

- Creative accounting doesn't add up.

- Pyramids are popular.

- In government speak, "hanky-panky" means "business as usual."

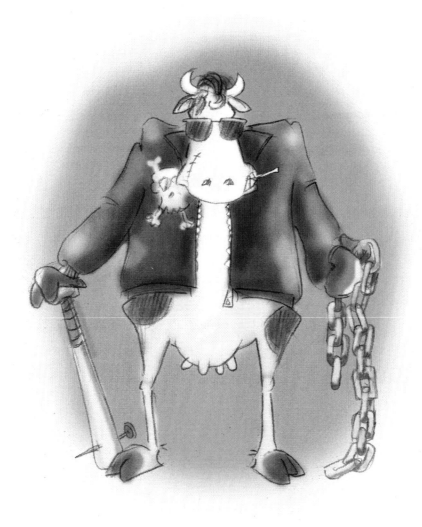

# Reprogramming Activities

## Activity #1—Giving the USDA Recommendations a Go!

The USDA pyramid is about as confusing as taxes. Unfortunately, our taxes paid to build that pyramid, so we might as well try to get something from it.

Here's how we'll do it. For a whole day, check off everything you eat in its appropriate column. Remember, a cheeseburger isn't a food group, so if you have one, break it down. The bun is a couple ounces of bread, so make 2 checks in the Grains column. The burger is 3 or 4 ounces of meat, so that's 3 or 4 checks in the meat column. If you have a beer and some chips with your cheeseburger, then that's a few checks in the All the Other Crap You Eat column (a.k.a. Discretionary Calories), and so on.

Just like the food log from the last chapter, include everything you eat for the day. By the end of the day, notice what you're getting enough or too much of (probably White Grains and All the Other Crap You Eat), and what you're not getting enough of (probably Fruits and Vegetables).

If you're a woman, use the first chart. It's based on USDA recommendations for a 2,000-calorie-a-day diet, which, it says, is about right for most moderately active women under 50 (moderately active = walking 1.5 to 3 miles a day). If you're over 50, or under 50 and sedentary, sorry, you have to eat a little less (around 1,800 calories). If you're over 50 and sedentary, it drops again (1,600 calories). Hey, no one said getting old is fun.

If you're a man, use the second chart. It's based on USDA recommendations for a 2,600-calorie-a-day diet, which, it says, is about right for most moderately active men under 50. Over 50, or under 50 and sedentary, it drops to around 2,200. Over 50 and sedentary, it drops to 2,000.

Keep in mind those crazy government measurements. A cup of rice is 2 government ounces, so if you have two cups of rice with lunch, that's 4 government ounces (4 of your 6 servings). Refer back to the chapter (or to "Inside the Pyramid" at the Mypyramid website for even more examples) if you need some help.

117

## 2,000 CALORIE CHECKLIST

| GRAINS | VEGETABLES | FRUITS | MILK | MEAT & BEANS | ALL THE OTHER CRAP YOU EAT |
|---|---|---|---|---|---|
| 6 ounce equivalents | 2 ½ cups | 2 cups | 3 cups | 5 ½ ounce equivalents | Limit to 265 calories |
| —— | —— | —— | —— | —— | —— |
| —— | —— | —— | —— | —— | —— |
| —— | —— | —— | —— | —— | —— |
| —— | —— | —— | —— | —— | —— |
| —— | —— | —— | —— | —— | —— |
| —— | —— | —— | —— | —— | —— |
| —— | —— | —— | —— | —— | —— |
| —— | —— | —— | —— | —— | —— |
| —— | —— | —— | —— | —— | —— |
| —— | —— | —— | —— | —— | —— |
| —— | —— | —— | —— | —— | —— |
| —— | —— | —— | —— | —— | —— |
| —— | —— | —— | —— | —— | —— |
| —— | —— | —— | —— | —— | —— |
| —— | —— | —— | —— | —— | —— |
| —— | —— | —— | —— | —— | —— |

118

## 2,600 CALORIE CHECKLIST

| GRAINS | VEGETABLES | FRUITS | MILK | MEAT & BEANS | ALL THE OTHER CRAP YOU EAT |
|---|---|---|---|---|---|
| 9 ounce equivalents | 3 ½ cups | 2 cups | 3 cups | 6 ½ ounce equivalents | Limit to 410 calories |
| —— | —— | —— | —— | —— | —— |
| —— | —— | —— | —— | —— | —— |
| —— | —— | —— | —— | —— | —— |
| —— | —— | —— | —— | —— | —— |
| —— | —— | —— | —— | —— | —— |
| —— | —— | —— | —— | —— | —— |
| —— | —— | —— | —— | —— | —— |
| —— | —— | —— | —— | —— | —— |
| —— | —— | —— | —— | —— | —— |
| —— | —— | —— | —— | —— | —— |
| —— | —— | —— | —— | —— | —— |
| —— | —— | —— | —— | —— | —— |
| —— | —— | —— | —— | —— | —— |
| —— | —— | —— | —— | —— | —— |
| —— | —— | —— | —— | —— | —— |
| —— | —— | —— | —— | —— | —— |

## Activity #2—Balance and Portions

There are simpler ways to make sure we get better balance and variety in our diets, while also keeping an eye on how much we eat. To find out which way might work best for you, take my Short Personality Quiz.

### SHORT PERSONALITY QUIZ

1. When watching TV, I always check out what's on...

    a.  ESPN

    b.  DIY Network

    c.  NASA TV

2. I can't wait to visit....

    a.  the Pro Football Hall of Fame

    b.  my local weekend crafts fair

    c.  Mars

3. If headed to a casual Saturday BBQ, I'll most likely throw on...

    a.  my favorite professional sports jersey

    b.  some special piece of handmade jewelry to jazz up my summer dress

    c.  a spacesuit

4. On eBay, I'm most likely to bid on...

    a.  autographed sports memorabilia

    b.  artisan crafts

    c.  moon dust

5. If I could have dinner with any celebrity, I'd pick...

    a.  Brett Favre

    b.  Martha Stewart

    c.  E.T.

If you answered mostly A, you're probably a sports fan.
**See The Game Plan.**

If you answered mostly B, you're probably a creative person.
**See The Hand Plan.**

If you answered mostly C, you're probably a trekkie.
**See The Space Plan.**

Let's start with The Game Plan.

## The Game Plan

A sports fan like you probably loves details, so long as they have to do with last night's game. You may not even own a set of measuring cups, but you've got balls, clubs, cards, and dice. Perfect. You can use those to help you keep score. For example:

- A cup of rice is about the same size as a tennis ball.
- A regular bagel is about the same size as a hockey puck.
- Three ounces of meat is about the same size as a deck of cards.
- One ounce of cheese is about the same size as a pair of dice.

Notice nothing is about the same size as a football or a basketball. Here's how the Game Plan works. First, get a plate. Next, get a tennis ball and a deck of cards, and put them on your plate. The deck of cards represents approximately how big your portion of protein should be at each meal, and the tennis ball represents approximately how big your portion of grains or starches should be. For example, let's say you want some chicken and rice. All you have to remember is a deck-of-cards-sized piece of chicken and a tennis-ball-sized portion of rice.

Love steak and potatoes? Fine. Have a deck-of-cards-sized piece of steak and a tennis-ball-sized portion of potatoes. You may be thinking, "I can eat a steak three times that size," and that's just dandy. Hot-dog-eating legend Takeru Kobayashi can eat 50 hot dogs in twelve minutes, which goes to show, just because you can do something doesn't mean you need to, especially if there's no prize involved.

What do you do with all that extra space on your plate? Fill it up with vegetables, like lettuce, tomatoes, cauliflower, onions, peppers, broccoli, and carrots, to name a few.

How do you work a big bowl of pasta and a basket of garlic bread into the game plan? You don't—unless your game plan is to be a sumo wrestler.

## The Hand Plan

If you're a creative, crafty person, The Hand Plan may be right for you. That's right—your very own hands can help you create a balanced, well-portioned meal.

First, hold out one of your hands, make a fist and look at it. This is about how big your stomach is. It can hold as much as it does because it's made of spandex. Next, hold your hand out flat and look at your palm. This is about what one serving of meat looks like, so:

- Your palm is approximately the size of three ounces of meat (⅔ of your palm if you're a man).

- Your fist is approximately the size of a cup or 8 ounces of cereal (⅔ of your fist if you're a man).

- Your cupped hand is about the size of ½ cup or 4 ounces of pasta.

- Two thumbs together are about the size of a tablespoon.

- The tip of your thumb is about the size of a teaspoon.

In general, here's how The Hand Plan works: the palm of your hand represents approximately how big your portion of protein should be at each meal and your fist represents approximately how big your portion of grains or starches should be. So the pattern for your plan at each meal is a palm-sized portion of protein (meat, fish, poultry, beans, eggs) and a fist-sized portion of grains or starches (bread, cereal, pasta, potatoes, rice). Add a colorful variety of vegetables to complete your creation and enjoy.

# The Space Plan

If you're the scientific type who loves to stare at stars and contemplate the earth's real age, The Space Plan may be for you. For you, your plate is your planet, back when planets were flat.

What do you do with your flat planet? First, visualize an equator splitting it in two. Next, visualize 0° longitude running from your planet's North Pole to your planet's South Pole. Your flat planet is now divided into four equal regions. When it's time to eat, fill one region with protein, one region with grains or starches, and two regions with vegetables. Now, just because you've got one region of grains or starches doesn't mean you can pile a Mt. Everest of pasta there. Recommended elevation for your whole planet is about ½ inch above sea level. If you don't know how to fill two regions with vegetables, try one region of salad and a region of cooked vegetables (don't flood either of them in an ocean of ranch dressing).

You'll notice the previous plans have a lot in common with one another and very little in common with a triple-decker cheeseburger and half a plate of fries. But if you replace that triple-decker cheeseburger with a regular hamburger, skip the fries (your bun is starch enough) and have half a plate of salad (watch the dressing, of course), that's not so bad, is it?

Whichever plan you choose, remember:

- Lean proteins, like skinless poultry, are better than high-fat proteins, like fried chicken.

- Whole grains, like brown rice, are better than refined grains, like white rice.

- A cup of broccoli has about 50 calories. A cup of broccoli with a cup of melted cheese on top has about 1,000 calories.

- Being saucy is fun. Being sauced is fun (as long as you're not driving). Being covered in sauce is fattening.

- Just because salmon is good for you doesn't mean you need a pound of it.

Try The Game Plan, The Hand Plan or The Space Plan at your very next meal. If you're out to eat, try to stick to it too (that probably means you won't be finishing your plate, so take the extra home). Remember, your plan, which is to eat less, is not the same as the restaurant's plan, which is to sell you more food. When you're finished, check all that apply:

☐ I did it!
☐ I didn't exactly do it.
☐ I got confused and ate a deck of cards.
☐ What's for dessert?
☐ I just want to read the book.

## Activity #3—Snack Exchange

Having a fist-sized portion of rice at lunch and dinner won't make much difference if you snack on an arm-sized hoagie in between. Snacks aren't off-limits, but they shouldn't be larger than your meal. They should also offer you something besides sugar and salt, so for a whole day, skip the junk food snacks and exchange them for something more natural, like fruit.

## Activity #4—A Food Heart

Whether it's meal time or snack time, we can all benefit from eating fewer high-fat, high-sugar, salty, processed foods. Copy this food heart and carry it with you. Inside it are the WHO's basic diet recommendations for all of us (basically). Throughout the day, as you go through the cafeteria line or stand in front of the vending machine, pull this heart out and let it help you guide your choices.

**More Fruits, Vegetables, Legumes (Beans), Whole Grains and Nuts.**

**Fewer Sugars, Salt, and Total Fats.**

## Activity #5—Get Porn Out of the House

I'm talking about food porn (bad fats and sugars). Your sex life is your own business. To get food porn out of your house, go to your kitchen and throw out all the high-fat, high-sugar treats you have stashed everywhere. If all you have to snack on is an apple, you'll snack on an apple. If you have to choose between an apple and chocolate chip cookies, you'll pick chocolate chip cookies every time.

## Activity #6—Stop Vegetablism!

Vegetablism is the unfair discrimination against vegetables. Do your part to stop vegetablism by eating more of them today. If buying fresh vegetables isn't an option for you, buy frozen vegetables (which are sometimes fresher than what's sitting out in the produce aisle) or juice. Start now. Have a Bloody Mary.

These growth hormones really work.

# CHAPTER 6

# The Good, the Bad, and the Toxic

## Why Do We Eat?

Let's keep at the reprogramming process by answering the following question:

I eat for _____.

There are no right or wrong answers. Some possible answers might include:

**I eat for fun.**

**I eat for taste.**

**I eat for six.**

**Who needs for a reason?**

Turns out we can eat for any reason we want, but we have to eat to live. Food is what keeps our blood pumping, our lungs breathing, our eyes blinking. Food is also what keeps our body growing. You may think that as an adult, it's a done deal, but our body is constantly rebuilding and replacing things. Let's face it. None of us just drove off the lot. That's why we have to help our body rebuild and replace things by eating the right kinds of food. If we don't, we may end up in the shop for a major overhaul, like a triple bypass.

Food is what allows our body to exert itself, like when we run up the stairs to get in the beer line before halftime. That's why when we go on any of those no-calorie diets, we can't get off the floor. We need food. We need the calories from it and the nutrients in it to keep our machine running properly. Knowing this, why would anyone stuff it with crap? It doesn't make sense. It only makes sense if somehow we've forgotten what food does, and I think perhaps some of us have. So let's look at what food does and how it does it.

Let's start with where food goes. This may seem obvious, but what the heck. Most people think food just goes into their mouth, then to their tummy, then through a long tunnel, and then out the back. This is correct. But food isn't just passing through. It's being worked for all it's got. And who's doing the work? We are, first with our mouths, where we grind it with our teeth and mix it with saliva to break it down, then with our stomachs where we mash it into slush and attack the bad germs with acid. Next we work it with our intestines, first in the small intestines, where we leach out the nutrients and absorb them into our bloodstream, and then in the large intestines where we squeeze out whatever's left (mostly water and salt) before sending it to the pooper where we discard the waste.

Okay, so it's not the most scientific explanation, but you get the idea. The point is, when we eat, our body goes into high gear to get every bit of nourishment it can from the food we feed it. Imagine how disappointed it must be when it goes through all that work for nothing.

*Thou shouldst eat to live; not live to eat.*

—SOCRACTES

*Either way, clean up after yourself.*

—LISA PEDACE

## The Nutrients

There are six essential nutrients the body is working so hard to get. They are carbohydrates, fats, protein, water, vitamins, and minerals.

Despite what we've been brainwashed to believe, we need all of six of these nutrients in the right amounts. We need carbohydrates, fats, protein, and water in larger amounts, which is why they are referred to as macronutrients, and vitamins and minerals in smaller, sometimes only trace amounts, which is why they are referred to as micronutrients. Fiber, a carbohydrate we hear so much of lately, isn't on the list because our body doesn't absorb it, which is exactly why it's useful for moving things along.

If, in the past, you've found nutrition talk complicated, you are not alone. Probably one of the reasons it seems complicated is because, like a lot of food talk, it seems to change often. This is not your imagination. How the body works and what the body needs is sort of one of those, "the more we know, the less we know" conundrums. Or maybe it's "the more we know, the less we agree." It could be "the more we know, the less we remember," or even, "the more we know, the less we'll admit." Whatever it is, it can be difficult to get a handle on. And of course, the government can't be trusted. Since I'm not a nutritionist, I can hardly be trusted either, but I'll do my best.

## Carbohydrates

Let's start with everyone's favorite, carbohydrates.

**Carbohydrates are the body's main source of energy.**

If you need some energy, you can eat some carbohydrates and, voilà, problem solved. If you don't need some energy, you can eat some carbohydrates and, voilà, your body will convert them into fat and put them in your closet for later. When your closet is full, your body will put them under your bed. When the space under your bed is full, your body will put them behind your couch. When the space behind your couch is full, your body will put them in the corner, and so on. Eventually nothing fits anywhere anymore.

Like people, there are different kinds of carbohydrates in the world. Some are simple, some are complex, some, like fiber, are just passing through, but they all have one thing in common: the sugar molecule.

Simple carbohydrates like candy, fruit, and milk have one or two chains of this molecule. Complex carbohydrates, like cereal grains, rice, beans, and some vegetables—potatoes, carrots, peas, and corn—have multiple chains. Our body breaks both simple and complex carbohydrates back down into the basic sugar molecule for energy. The difference between the two is in how quickly they're absorbed into the bloodstream. Simple sugars are converted quickly and complex carbohydrates are converted more slowly.

Does that mean that all simple carbohydrates are bad or, conversely, that all complex carbohydrates are good? No. It's all about what else we're getting. When it comes to simple carbohydrates, fruit's a better choice than cotton candy because fruit gives us other important nutrients, like vitamins and fiber. Cotton candy gives us sticky fingers and a toothache.

It's the same thing with complex carbohydrates. Some give us more than others. Whole grains (like whole wheat bread) give us more than processed grains (like white sandwich bread), and because they take longer to digest, we feel fuller longer (useful when we're trying to lose weight).

As you can see, nutrients aren't the same thing as food groups. Here in carbohydrates, we have milk, fruits, and even table sugar right along with breads, cereals, and grains. If you're getting more confused by the paragraph, don't feel bad. Sometimes science and government don't mix. Sometimes science and science don't even mix, as evidenced by a fairly recent newcomer known as the Glycemic Index.

# The Glycemic Index

If you pay any attention to diet talk, you've probably heard of the Glycemic Index. First developed as a tool for diabetics, the Glycemic Index gives carbohydrates a numeric value based on how fast they're converted into sugars. These numbers fall into three classifications: low, medium, and high. Carbohydrates with a low GI, 55 or less, release more slowly than carbohydrates with a high GI, 70 or more. An apple has a GI of 36, which makes it a low GI food. A pineapple has a GI of 66, making it a medium GI food. A Snickers candy bar has a GI anywhere from 40-60. (I hate when the experts can't agree.) Does that mean a Snickers bar is a better choice than pineapple?

To counter some of the confusion associated with the Glycemic Index, the Glycemic Load has been added to the mix. The Glycemic Load, or GL, is the new number that Glycemic Groupies, or GGs, like to get excited about. The GL is found by some special accounting that takes into consideration the original GI and then factors in other factors (yes, I meant to write that) like the amount of carbohydrate in a certain food, and the amount of that food one might actually eat. You might think this would have been part of the initial formula, but it wasn't. That's the problem with science: it's always trying to catch up with itself. The end result is that pineapple is a better choice than a Snickers bar, after all. But you already knew that, didn't you? We'll wrap up carbohydrates with this important fact:

**Carbohydrates are an essential part of a healthy diet for the energy they provide, but eat too many of them and the extra gets stored as fat.**

This is as true for stone-ground whole-grain whole-wheat bread as it is for chocolate donuts. In other words, you don't need to carbo-load on either of them to sit at your desk for eight hours.

# Fats

Fats have gotten a bad rap over the years, but everybody needs them. Fats are not just important for the extra stored energy they provide; they are also necessary for the absorption of certain vitamins. Not only that, fats support, protect, and insulate our organs. But not all fats are created equal.

**Like witches, some fats are good and some fats are bad.**

Good fats include monounsaturated fatty acids (MUFAs) and poly-unsaturated fatty acids (PUFAs), which are found in plant food and fish. Bad fats include saturated fats, also known as saturated fatty acids (SFAs), which are found in meat and other animal products like milk and cheese, and trans fats, or trans-isomer fatty acids (TFAs), used in fried food, snack food, and baked goods, which are MUFAs and PUFAs that have under-gone a chemical process to make them live longer. That's right. They're witches from another planet.

# Cholesterol

To better understand why some fats are good and some fats are bad, we have to bring up their misunderstood cousin, cholesterol.

Cholesterol is a waxy fat-like substance, belonging to the steroid family, that the liver makes and the body needs for a couple of important func-tions, including the production of vitamin D, the construction of cell walls, and the formation of some hormones, especially the sexy ones. Our body already makes plenty of cholesterol, but it gets extra from the food we eat that comes from animal sources like meats, eggs, and dairy products.

**The cholesterol in our body is called blood cholesterol and the cholesterol we eat is called dietary cholesterol.**

Dietary cholesterol can raise our blood cholesterol, and too much cholesterol in our blood can lead to big problems. The reason has to do with the way it moves through our bodies. In fact, it doesn't move on its own at all because cholesterol, like other fats, doesn't dissolve in our blood. To get where it's going, it needs a little help from its friends, called lipoproteins.

The main lipoproteins are LDL (low-density lipoprotein) and HDL (high-density lipoprotein). LDL is the main carrier of cholesterol in our bodies, which would be fine if LDL weren't so lazy. When LDL has too much to move, he doesn't work harder or longer, he just starts dropping boxes of cholesterol in the hallways of our arteries. Our blood can barely squeeze by to get to the computer. Too many boxes and the whole artery clogs up. Then we have a heart attack.

HDL is the other mover on the block and, boy, does he work hard. He doesn't just drop boxes willy-nilly wherever he pleases. He carries them all the way back to our livers where our livers can process them and move them out. That's why we want to increase the amount of HDL working for us, and decrease the amount of LDL working against us. Eating the right kinds of fats (in the right amounts) can help us do that.

Monounsaturated fats and polyunsaturated fats increase our hard-working HDL and decrease our lazy LDL. This is why they're good fats. Saturated fats increase both our HDL and our LDL. This is why they're bad fats. Trans fats (the worst) not only increase our lazy LDL, they also decrease our hardworking HDL. This is why they're evil alien fats.

## Protein

Another must-have! Without protein, we can't put Humpty Dumpty back together again. We sit on a wall and have a great fall; we're out of luck if our body isn't getting any protein.

**Proteins build and repair our body tissues.**

When we eat protein, our body breaks it down into building blocks called amino acids, then our body gets to work, rebuilding these amino acids into new proteins that get sent to our muscles, organs, and whatever else we're remodeling at any given moment. Some amino acids are nonessential, meaning our body makes them, and others are essential, meaning we have to get them from the food we eat.

If you eat any kind of animal protein, as in meat, seafood, poultry, eggs or dairy, you don't really have to worry about amino acids; all these foods are complete proteins, meaning they've got the essentials covered. Nuts, seeds, legumes, grains, and vegetables are all good sources of incomplete proteins that can be paired up nicely to create complete proteins if you wake up vegetarian one day. What's important to know about protein is that our body doesn't store amino acids the way it stores carbohydrates and fat, so we need a little every day.

For the record, protein has 4 calories per gram. Carbohydrates also have 4 calories per gram. Fat has 9 calories per gram, and alcohol has 7 calories per gram. This is the kind of nutritional information that screws up a lot of people because they think it means a pound of pasta is better than a pat of butter. Is it? It depends who you ask. People selling you the "no fat, lots of carbs" diet will tell you one thing, while people selling you the "no carbs, lots of fat" diet will tell you something else. People selling you the "lots of love, lots of wine" diet will tell you another thing entirely. Common sense tells me we need some amount of all of them every day. What does common sense tell you? So what do you do with that "calories per gram" information? Use it commonsensibly. Use it to remind you that something high in fat, like butter, is going to have more calories, so you don't need a lot of it. Though that still doesn't mean you need a pound of pasta.

## Water

Our last macronutrient is water, which has 0 calories per gram. You'd think at 0 calories per gram, water would be a big hit with dieters, but it's not, probably because you can't eat it. Still, we need some every day. Water is so important that we can't live without it. Food we can live without, probably up to 5 weeks. No water and we're dead in days. It makes you wonder why water didn't get a spot on the pyramid. Oh yeah, I forgot. You have to pay for those. In this country, sort-of clean drinking water is free, which is another reason it should be a hit with dieters, but it isn't, probably because you can't eat it.

The human body is made up of about 75% water. If visuals help you understand things better, imagine there's a big log ride inside you. Without water, the log ride doesn't function, but with water, the ride flourishes. Water keeps the logs moving, the system clean, the kiddies cool. No water and the ride shuts down and dries up in the summer heat. Little Billy's crying because he's too hot.

**Water cools, cleans, and transports stuff through your body.**

Water does lots of other important things too, like make us sweat when we go on interviews and dates. It's also good for getting down really dry crackers. Besides drinking water and other liquids, we get water from many of the foods we eat. However we get it, we will shrivel up and die without it. Does that mean we should walk around with a water bottle hanging around our neck? No. It just means if we're thirsty we should drink some water. Will drinking water give us beautiful skin, a thinner physique and a better personality? Look, it's a nutrient, not a miracle drink. Do we have to drink expensive bottled water? No. I know the bottled water industry (and fancy restaurants) like to make us feel like feral cats for drinking tap water, but that's just to sell us an expensive bottle of something we can get free. Yes, I know it has some problems, but we'll be long dead from something else before regular tap water kills us (like maybe the toxins that leaked from the plastic bottle into the bottled water because somebody left the whole shipment on the dock for a week in Santa Ana heat).

## The Micronutrients

Vitamins and minerals are both micronutrients that our body needs in small amounts to do whatever it does when we're not looking, the list of which I can't even imagine.

It used to be we didn't have to worry about vitamins and minerals too much as long as we were eating a varied diet. Then it got to be that we didn't have to worry too much about eating a varied diet as long as we were taking a daily multivitamin. Now it turns out there are very important things called phytochemicals. Phytochemicals are powerful antioxidants that may protect us from the bad oxidizing effects of this dirty world we live in.

The thing about phytochemicals is that they're only found in plant substances (phyto equals plant), like fruits and vegetables, and some beans and grains. That means we actually have to go back to eating these foods to get their beneficial phytochemicals.

Because they are so beneficial, scientists are working round the clock to figure out the best way to put them into pill form. Then we won't have to worry about phytochemicals either. We'll just be able to pop a multivitamin / mineral / phytochemical pill in our mouths and get on with our day. I personally prefer food to pills, but that's just me and I'm Italian.

The mineral sodium (street name: salt) is worth a special mention because it's such a troublemaker. First of all, it bloats us like a beached whale. More importantly, it's linked to high blood pressure, which is the leading cause of stroke. High blood pressure also contributes to heart attack, heart failure, and kidney failure.

The surprising thing about sodium is that it shows up in unexpected places. We all know, for example, that fast food is high in sodium (one Big Mac has over 1,000 milligrams of sodium), but did you know a cup of regular cottage cheese can have almost as much? That's why we have to go beyond what we think we know about food (and what people tell us about food) and actually *read the labels*.

## Nutrition Facts and Ingredient List

So here it is again: the predominantly placed (by law) and in a white box (also by law) Nutrition Facts label. This is our same macaroni & cheese label from Chapter 4, which I got from the FDA website. Let's take another look at it. What do you know? So many of the things we're supposed to be paying attention to are right there on the label for us to see.

We've already mentioned serving size, servings per container and calories per serving, so let's see what else is there.

# Nutrition Facts

Serving Size 1 cup (228g)
Servings Per Container  2

**Amount Per Serving**

**Calories** 250          Calories from Fat 110

| | % Daily Value* |
|---|---|
| **Total Fat** 12g | 18% |
| Saturated Fat 3g | 15% |
| *Trans* Fat 3g | |
| **Cholesterol** 30mg | 10% |
| **Sodium** 470mg | 20% |
| **Total Carbohydrate** 31g | 10% |
| Dietary Fiber 0g | 0% |
| Sugars 5g | |
| **Protein** 5g | |
| Vitamin A | 4% |
| Vitamin C | 2% |
| Calcium | 20% |
| Iron | 4% |

You'll notice as we proceed down the label that there's a column on the left and a column on the right. The column on the left lists the different nutrients we've been talking about, plus how much there is of each nutrient per serving in whatever we're eating. Take Total Fat, for example. On our example label, we see that one serving of this food has 12 grams of total fat. But how much is that? Enough? Too much! Not enough? To help us understand it better, we simply look at the column on the right. This column is entitled % Daily Value. On our label, we see that:

|                   | % Daily Value |
| ----------------- | ------------- |
| **Total Fat 12g** | **18%**       |

The USDA recommends that we get less than 65 grams of total fat per day (based on a 2,000 calorie intake). The % Daily Value tells us how much of that this particular serving is going to give us. We don't even have to do the math. They've done it for us. According to this label, 12 grams of fat is 18% of the fat we need for the day. If we eat the whole pack (2 servings) we've had 18% times 2 or 36% of the fat we need for the day.

> **A Daily Value of 5% or less is low.**
> **A Daily Value of 20% or more is high.**

You'll notice that Trans Fat doesn't have a Daily Value. That's because "experts could not provide a reference value" for them. In other words, the government knows they're bad for us, but it likes to keep its friends. It's the same deal with Sugar. Protein doesn't have a Daily Value either because, as I already explained, Milk and Meat have good agents.

Now, just because something has low % Daily Values doesn't necessarily mean it's any better for our health. Foods can be low in fat, cholesterol, and sodium, and still be nutritional vacuums (can you say soda?), so when you go shopping, bring your head. You'll need it to make decisions.

Perhaps more telling than the Nutrition Facts label is the Ingredient List, which is also included, begrudgingly, by law. Find it and read it too. You may be surprised to learn how little food is actually in some foods these days.

---

**Ingredients are listed in descending order
of predominance and weight, so the sooner you see it listed,
the more there is of it inside.**

---

Are there good ingredients and bad ingredients? Certainly. As a general rule, I guess we could say that if we've heard of it and it sounds like food, it's probably a better bet than if we've never heard of it and it sounds like a laboratory, but even this isn't cut and dry.

Whether it's food or not, if it's in there, it's gotten the nod from the FDA. What's that mean for us? Hardly anything. Over the years, the FDA has given the go-ahead for all sorts of things that might kill us. Fortunately, there are other groups who pay attention to some of this stuff, like the Center for Science in the Public Interest, for example.

## THE CSPI

The Center for Science in the Public Interest, or the CSPI, is one of those consumer watchdog groups that likes to whoop and holler. It whoops and hollers over vending machines in middle schools; it whoops and hollers over alcohol ads during televised college sports; it whoops and hollers over fat in restaurant and takeout food. In addition to whooping and hollering, the CSPI wants to sue and tax people too. Not poor slops like you and me, but the rich food and restaurant slops who will sell anything to anyone regardless of how quickly it will kill you. I say cheers to the CSPI for bringing some of this of our attention. Are they right about everything? Who knows? But I'd trust the watchdog over the security guard any day. It's harder to bribe a watchdog.

A few of the additives the CSPI suggests we avoid include:

- **Acesulfame K** (also known as acesulfame potassium), an artificial sweetener, found in baked goods, chewing gum, gelatin desserts, and soft drinks, which may cause cancer.

- **Aspartame**, another artificial sweetener found in diet soft drinks, diet drink mixes, diet gelatin desserts, low-calorie frozen desserts, and sugar substitute packets, which may cause cancer.

- **Hydrogenated and partially hydrogenated oils**, plant oils that have been chemically treated to extend shelf life, found in margarine, crackers, fried restaurant foods, and baked goods, that promote heart disease.

- **Potassium bromate**, a flour improver found in bread and rolls that may cause cancer and has been banned in most of the world except the US and Japan.

- **Saccharine**, one more artificial sweetener, found in diet foods, sugar substitute packets and diet soft drinks (including fountain diet drinks at restaurants), which may cause cancer.

How much proof is there that these things are dangerous to humans? Who knows? The human studies (thank you for your participation) are still in progress. Let's just say a lot of rats have suffered so you can have a diet soda. And artificial sweeteners aren't just in "diet" food. They can be anywhere, like in "light" yogurt, or "sugar-free" pudding or ice cream.

Meanwhile, hydrogenated and partially hydrogenated oils and potassium bromate are used in a lot of the foods that make controlling our weight so difficult. That's why, whether we're dieting or not, we have to pay attention to what we're eating.

For the record, the CSPI also wants us to avoid caffeine and hot dogs, so you can see why they don't have many friends. If you go to their website (cspinet.org), you'll find a whole list of additives and their position on each one. Read it and then—you got it—decide for yourself.

## Organic vs. Nonorganic

As you start to pay more attention to what your food says, you'll no doubt notice the ever-expanding variety of organic products available. What does "organic food" mean? According to the USDA Consumer Brochure, *Organic Food Standards and Labels: The Facts*:

> Organic food is produced by farmers who emphasize the use of renewable resources and the conservation of soil and water to enhance environmental quality for future generations. Organic meat, poultry, eggs, and dairy products come from animals that are given no antibiotics or growth hormones. Organic food is produced without using most conventional pesticides, fertilizers made with synthetic ingredients or sewage sludge, bioengineering, or ionizing radiation. Before a product can be labeled "organic," a government-approved certifier inspects the farm where the food is grown to make sure the farmer is following all the rules necessary to meet USDA organic standards. Companies that handle or process organic food before it gets to your local supermarket or restaurant must be certified, too.

That's right. The government decides what gets to be organic. In the beginning, this, like every other time the government has decided to regulate something, seemed like a good idea. I mean, you wouldn't want just anybody to slap the word "organic" on something, especially since organic also means more expensive. Everybody would do it. That's why, in 2002, the USDA implemented government standards. What did Milk and Meat do? They got their agents on the phone.

"$5.00 for a gallon a milk?" Milk said. "Count us in. Everybody should drink organic milk. The only problem is we don't have enough organic cows."

Not to worry. According to the USDA, cows only have to start living organic once they arrive at the organic milk-making facility. That means you can juice them up with antibiotics and growth hormones before they get there. I'm not saying that's what anybody does. I'm just saying organic dairy farms don't have to do background checks on their cows. And according to *Consumer Reports*, there are other loopholes too. Organically raised animals are supposed to have access to the outdoors, but that doesn't necessarily mean cows are roaming around freely. They may just be cramped together in an outdoor pen. And for "organic" chickens, the rules are even sketchier. Their "outdoor access" might be nothing more than a coop with a window.

That's like paying for an ocean view room, but having to stand on the toilet to see it. Does that mean organic food is a crock? Not

yet, but large food manufacturers are working on it.

And what about that "organic milk?" Not a bad idea, according to *Consumer Reports*. Why? Because regular cows are so juiced up, they should play baseball. *Consumer Reports* also recommends buying organic meat, poultry, eggs, and baby food whenever possible. And yes, it will cost more, but it's all in the way you look at it. In other words, don't think, "Organic costs more." Think, "Chemicals cost less."

Organic seafood you can skip because the government hasn't gotten to fish—yet. That means the seafood industry can slap "organic" on anything they want, but as long as they don't slap "USDA" or "certified organic" on it, there's not much anyone is going to do about it.

Organic fruits and vegetables can be a good choice in some cases, but not all, including the case that the store you shop at doesn't stock them. If that's the case, you can still control your exposure to chemicals you don't want—in this case, pesticides—by avoiding certain fruits and vegetables that tend to have higher doses.

According to the nonprofit advocacy Environmental Working Group (EWG), the fruits and vegetables that currently have the highest levels of pesticide residues are peaches, apples, bell peppers, celery, nectarines, strawberries, cherries, kale, lettuce, imported grapes, carrots, and pears. These are what EWG call the "Dirty Dozen," so if you can buy these things organic, it's not a bad idea in their book. If you can't buy these things organic, you might want to eat more onions, avocados, and sweet corn. That's because these foods, according to the EWG, have the lowest levels of pesticide residues. Other "clean" fruits and vegetables include pineapples, mangoes, asparagus, sweet peas, kiwi, cabbage, eggplant, papaya, watermelon, broccoli, tomatoes, and sweet potatoes. Check out their website for more info (www.ewg.org) and for subsequent Best and Worst Dressed Lists.

And what about organic when it comes to packaged foods, like canned or dried fruits and vegetables, or breads, cereals, crackers, pasta, potato chips, and oils? *Consumer Reports* says it's up to you. If you're feeling flush, go for it, but these products can lose a lot of their "organic" benefits through processing.

143

## What Cigarettes Have Taught Us

What cigarettes have taught us is that just because we can buy something off a shelf doesn't mean it's good for our health. Cigarettes have also taught us that even when we know something is bad for our health, we may still buy it. In other words, maybe the government doesn't care any less than we do.

If we really want to reprogram ourselves, we must start to care. Get in the habit of reading the Nutrition Facts label and the Ingredients List when you can and look for food that has food in it. Look for food that has more nutrients and less added fat, sugar, salt, preservatives, chemicals, and additives. If you don't care, you may pay the consequences. If you get fat and suffer a heart attack, the food and restaurant industry will not take up a collection to help you pay your medical bills. If you get cancer, the FDA and the diet industry won't help you either.

Along the way, realize that real food is not the enemy. Neither is information, although it tends to flip-flop a lot. Carbs are good, then they're bad, then they're teacher's pet. Protein is in, then it's out, then it's the new color for spring. Fat is the enemy, then it's an ally, then it's the new ambassador for food. Don't worry about the current popular standing of any of them. All of them are important to help your body function properly, and you can eat all of them in the right amounts. Instead, worry about what's being done to your food before it gets to your mouth.

> *The unexamined life is not worth living.*
>
> —SOCRATES

> *While you're at it, look at your plate.*
>
> —LISA PEDACE

# Let's Sum It Up

- Carbohydrates tend to pile up.

- Fats are like diamonds. Quality is everything.

- Largely made of water, people splat when dropped from high places.

- Your body is a good builder. Don't compromise the work with cheap supplies.

- Sometimes you're part of a test group and you don't even know it.

- Laboratory results often disappear.

- If salt were money, we'd all be rich.

- Some animals are on steroids.

# Reprogramming Activities

## Activity #1-Guess the Food

I've listed the ingredients. You try and guess what it is. The correct answers are at the end of the chapter.

1. Milk and Part-Skim Milk, Water, Whey, Milk fat, Sodium Phosphate, Contains Less Than 2% of Dried Corn Syrup, Salt, Worcestershire Sauce (Vinegar, Water, Molasses, Corn Syrup, Salt, Sugar, Caramel Color, Dried Garlic, Spice, Anchovies, Tamarino, Natural Preservative, Annatto (Color), Oleoresin Paprika, Enzymes.

2. Enriched Wheat Flour (Wheat Flour, Niacin, Reduced Iron, Thiamin Mononitrate, Riboflavin, Folic Acid), High Fructose Corn Syrup, Onion, Salt, Partially Hydrogenated Soybean and/or Cottonseed Oils, Cooked Chicken and Chicken Broth, Hydrolyzed Soy and Corn Protein, Yeast, Celery, Soy Flour, Monosodium Glutamate, Whey, Parsley Flakes, Spices, Sugar, Onion Powder, Caramel Color, Turmeric, Disodium Insinuate and Disodium Guanylate (Flavor Enhancers), Sodium Sulfite, BHA, BHT, Propyl Gallate and Citric Acid (Preservatives).

3. Non-Fat Milk, Water, Modified Corn Starch, Less Than 2% of: Partially Hydrogenated Soybean, Oil, Maltitol, Carrageenan, Artificial and Natural Flavors, Salt, Color Added (Including Yellow 5 and Yellow 6), Sodium Stearoyl Lactylate, Sucralose.

4. Maltitol, Enriched Flour (Wheat Flour, Niacin, Reduced Iron, Thiamine Mononitrate [Vitamin B1], Riboflavin [Vitamin B2], Folic Acid), High Oleic Canola Oil, Palm Oil, Polydextrose, Cocoa (Processed with Alkali), Cornstarch, Glycerin, Milk Protein Concentrate, Inulin (Natural Extract from Chicory Root), Whey Protein Concentrate, Emulsifiers (Vegetable Mono- and Diglycerides, Soy Lecithin), Leavening (Baking Soda, Monocalcium Phosphate, Sodium Acid Pyrophosphate), Salt, Milk (Enzyme Modified), Dextrose, Natural and Artificial Flavor, Cellulose Gum and Gel, Chocolate, Cream, Acesulfame Potassium (Sweetener), Sucralose (Sweetener).

5. Tomato Puree (Water, Tomato Paste), High Fructose Corn Syrup, Soybean Oil, Vinegar, Chopped Pickles, Salt, Contains less than 2% of Egg Yolks, Modified Food Starch, Water, Dried Onions, Xanthan Gum, Polysorbate 60, Phosphoric Acid, Spice, Artificial Color, Mustard Flour, with Potassium Sorbate and Calcium Disodium EDTA as Preservatives, Guar Gum, Natural Flavor, Oleoresin Turmeric, Yellow 5.

6. Black Beans, Water, and Salt.

7. Tomatoes (Water, Tomato Puree), Water, Enriched Wheat Flour (Wheat Flour, Malted Barley Flour, Niacin, Iron, Thiamine Mononitrate [Vitamin B1], Riboflavin [Vitamin B2], and Folic Acid), Beef, Crackermeal (Wheat Flour, Niacin, Iron, Thiamine Mononitrate [Vitamin B1], Riboflavin [Vitamin B2], and Folic Acid), Contains Less than 2% of: Salt, High Fructose Corn Syrup, Textured Vegetable Protein (Soy Flour, Soy Protein Concentrate and Caramel Coloring), Modified Corn Starch, Wheat Flour, Wheat Gluten, Carrots, Onions, Isolated Carrot Product, Monosodium Glutamate, Caramel Coloring, Flavorings, Enzyme Modified Cheese (Cheddar Cheese [Pasteurized Milk, Cultures, Salt, Enzymes], and Annatto [Color]), Soybean Oil and Citric Acid.

8. Whole Grain Corn, Sugar, Corn Syrup, Modified Corn Starch, Cocoa Processed with Alkali, Canola and/or Rice Bran Oil, Color Added, Salt, Fructose, Tricalcium Phosphate, Corn Starch, Natural and Artificial Flavor, Trisodium Phosphate, Wheat Flour, Vitamin E (Mixed Tocopherols) and BHT Added to Preserve Freshness. Vitamins and Minerals: Calcium Carbonate, Zinc and Iron (Mineral Nutrients), Vitamin C (Sodium Ascorbate), a B Vitamin (Niacinamide), Vitamin B6 (Pyridoxine Hydrochloride), Vitamin B2 (Riboflavin), Vitamin B1 (Thiamin Mononitrate), Vitamin A (Palmitate), a B Vitamin (Folic Acid), Vitamin B12, Vitamin D3.

9. Carbonated Water, Caramel Color, Aspartame, Phosphoric Acid, Potassium Benzoate (To Protect Taste), Natural Flavors, Citric Acid, Caffeine.

10. Filling (High Fructose Corn Syrup, Corn Syrup, Blueberry Puree Concentrate, Glycerin, Sugar, Modified Corn Starch, Sodium Alginate, Natural and Artificial Blueberry Flavor, Citric Acid, Sodium Citrate, Modified Cellulose, Dicalcium Phosphate, Malic Acid, Red No. 40, Blue No. 1), Enriched Flour (Wheat Flour, Niacinamide, Reduced Iron, Thiamin Mononitrate (Vitamin B1), Riboflavin (Vitamin B2), Folic Acid), Whole Grain Oats, Sugar, Sunflower Oil, High Fructose Corn Syrup, Contains Two Percent or Less of Honey, Calcium Carbonate, Dextrose, Nonfat Dry Milk, Wheat Bran, Salt, Cellulose, Potassium Bicarbonate (Leavening), Natural and Artificial Flavor, Mono- and Diglycerides, Propylene Glycol Esters of Fatty Acids, Soy Lecithin, Wheat Gluten, Cornstarch, Vitamin A Palmitate, Carrageenan, Niacinamide, Sodium Stearoyl Lactylate, Guar Gum, Zinc Oxide, Reduced Iron, Pyridoxine Hydrochloride (Vitamin B6), Thiamin Hydrochloride (Vitamin B1), Riboflavin (Vitamin B2), Folic Acid.

## Activity #2—Sugar Search

Sometimes there's more sugar in a product than you might think, but recognizing it means knowing some of the aliases it takes.

Take, for example, item number 8 from Activity #1. Sugar is the second ingredient listed, and corn syrup is the third. So not only is there sugar in that product, there's also corn syrup, which is sugar from corn.

Item number 10 is another example. That food contains high-fructose corn syrup, corn syrup, and sugar. That's sugar times three.

Here are some commonly used aliases for sugar. Next time you're out shopping, check to see if the food you're about to buy lists sugar more than once. Also, check to see if sugar is listed in the top three ingredients. If you want to buy food products that are loaded with sugar, plus some extra sugar by another name on top, that's up to you, but you might want to pick up some toothpaste while you're at it.

| | |
|---|---|
| high-fructose corn syrup | maltose |
| corn syrup | honey |
| corn sweetener | maple syrup |
| sucrose | malt syrup |
| fructose | molasses |
| glucose | syrup |
| dextrose | fruit juice concentrate |
| galactose | lactose |

## Activity #3–Sodium Match Game

The government might not want to give us a daily recommendation on how much sugar we should or shouldn't be consuming, but it gives us one for sodium. (I guess salt doesn't have the trade value it used to.) According to the USDA, we should all be getting less than 2,400 mg of sodium a day. Here are some sodium contents and some popular foods. See if you can match them up. The correct answers are at the end of the chapter.

| Sodium | | Food |
|---|---|---|
| 1. | 1,020 mg | Tostitos Medium All Natural Salsa–2 tbsp |
| 2. | 890 mg | Hot Pockets Frozen Food Ham and Cheese–1 pc |
| 3. | 190 mg | C and W Ultimate Petite Mixed Vegetables–¾ cup (frozen) |
| 4. | 420 mg | Heinz Ketchup Tomato–1 tbsp |
| 5. | 360 mg | Del Monte Peas and Carrots–½ cup (canned) |
| 6. | 70 mg | Banquet Chicken Fried Steak–1 meal |
| 7. | 260 mg | Kelloggs Eggo Buttermilk Waffles–2 waffles |
| 8. | 1,190 mg | Betty Crocker Lasagna Hamburger Helper–½ cup |
| 9. | 770 mg | Campbells Chicken Noodle Condensed Soup–½ cup |
| 10. | 820 mg | Digiorno Four Cheese For One Traditional Crust Pizza–1 pizza |

Next time you're out shopping, check the sodium content on everything you put in your cart. One thing you'll notice is that most convenience foods are loaded with it.

## Activity #4—Restaurant Reality Check

Speaking of USDA recommendations, here's the key to those USDA Daily Values we find on Nutrition Facts Labels. Like everything the government says and does, it's subject to change, but here's where it stands at the moment.

| Calories: | 2,000 | 2,600 |
|---|---|---|
| Total Fat | Less Than 65 g | 80 g |
| Saturated Fat | Less Than 20 g | 25 g |
| Cholesterol | Less Than 300 mg | 300mg |
| Sodium | Less Than 2,400 mg | 2,400mg |
| Total Carbohydrates | At Least 300 g | 375 g |
| Dietary Fiber | At Least 25 g | 30 g |

Remember our "Your Health Doesn't Matter to Us" Restaurant Calorie Quiz back in Chapter 5? Let's see how those menu items fare on some of these.

1. A Boneless Buffalo Chicken Salad from Chili's has 77 grams of fat and 4,380 mg of sodium.

2. A Parmesan Crusted Chicken entrée (no sides) from LongHorn Steakhouse has 69 grams of fat and 2,440 mg of sodium.

3. A regular Tuna Melt sandwich from Quiznos has 92 grams of fat and 1,510 mg of sodium.

4. A Veggie Quesadilla from Baja Fresh has 78 grams of fat and 2,310 mg of sodium.

5. A Sirloin Cheese Burger from Jack in the Box has 71 grams of fat and 2,040 mg of sodium.

6. A Crispy Calamari and Vegetables appetizer from Red Lobster has 98 grams of fat and 3,060 mg of sodium.

7. A Chicken and Shrimp Carbonara entrée from Olive Garden has 88 grams of fat and 3,000 mg of sodium.

8. A Carolina Chicken Salad from Ruby Tuesday has 68 grams of fat and, who knows how much sodium (they don't post sodium, yet).

Did I say restaurants don't care about your health? Hey, that doesn't mean they don't like you.

## Activity #5–Super Foods!

Now that you're paying more attention to what's in food, you're probably putting a lot of highly processed food items back on the shelf. If you find yourself at a loss for what to buy instead, you might want to consider some Super Foods! According to some doctors and nutritionists, super foods, like super heroes, pack an extra punch of nutrition. Unscramble the following words to learn what some of these super foods are. The correct answers are at the end of the chapter.

bereielursb _____        nniegtaesr _____

bracsnieerr _____        aslmno _____

rekibeclabsr _____        eimls _____

prraeiesbrs _____        cocirlob _____

erbserirswta _____        baabgce _____

gesroan _____        lsrubse usropts _____

sfireuratgp _____        gesg _____

thwea rgsas _____

upislnira_____

laohlrelc _____

lbyrae sagsr_____

chapsni_____

aelk _____

wssis acrdh _____

nmeiaro tlecetu _____

okb hyoc _____

crdallso _____

dderi nbsea _____

meeadam_____

serfh ngere ebnas _____

msonlda _____

rizbla tsnu _____

seapnc _____

nwsltua _____

aelomat _____

ato bnra _____

evisol _____

voile loi _____

dwil msanlo _____

unta _____

routt _____

eisndrsa _____

nmukpip _____

tnbttreuu hausqs _____

estwe opsaetot _____

sorrtca_____

mays_____

udsle _____

iiikjh_____

omukb_____

eaawkm _____

xflsseade _____

pknpmui essde_____

nlfwsuoer sdees _____

bsaynoes _____

ioylskm _____

yso tpnroei dwpero _____

rnege eta _____

wthie ate _____

cbalk aet _____

ognolo eta _____

aeosmtto _____

eyutrk _____

rbylea _____

yre_____

taewh _____

uygtro _____

rkeif _____

Do I eat all these foods? Not a chance. I haven't even heard of some of them. On a regular basis, I eat about ten to fifteen of them. Take another look at this list of foods, and circle ten or fifteen you could eat regularly. Don't pick things you don't like. The idea is to find foods you actually like so you actually eat them.

By the way, three of these foods show up on the EWG's "Dirty Dozen" list. That means they're Super Foods with a dark side.

## Activity #6—New & Improved Shopping List

Write five of the foods you circled from the last activity here.

1. _____

2. _____

3. _____

4. _____

5. _____

This is the beginning of your new and improved shopping list. Next time you go shopping, buy these five foods and incorporate them into your diet. And none of that "Eating better costs too much." Most of these items are cheaper than a lot of the processed foods many of us buy. Keep improving the quality of your shopping list (and your daily diet) by adding as many super foods to it as you can.

## Activity #7—Take a Walk through the Grocery Store

Some people suggest only shopping the perimeter of the store, which is where fresh produce, meat, and dairy are located. Of course, the bakery is usually there too, so it's not a foolproof plan. But there's nothing wrong with buying food in a can or a bag. Cans and bags aren't the problem. The problem is what's *added* to the food in the can or bag, which is usually a lot of flour, sugar, salt, starch, fat, artificial colors, and artificial flavors.

Next time you're at the store, take a leisurely walk through the aisles and look at how much shelf space is dedicated to highly processed, high-profit food. Eat before you do this or you might miss the point.

## Answers to Activity #1

1. Cheez Wiz
2. Stove Top Stuffing Mix, Chicken
3. Hunt's Snack Pack Pudding, Vanilla, No Sugar Added
4. Oreo Cookies, Carb Well
5. Kraft Salad Dressing, Thousand Island
6. Bush's Black Beans
7. Chef Boyardee Beef Ravioli in Tomato and Meat Sauce
8. General Mills Cocoa Puffs Cereal
9. Diet Coke
10. Kelloggs Snack Bars Nutrigrain Blueberry

## Answers to Activity #3

1. 1,020 mg Banquet Chicken Fried Steak–1meal
2. 890 mg Campbells Chicken Noodle Condensed Soup–½ cup
3. 190 mg Heinz Ketchup Tomato–1 tbsp
4. 420 mg Kelloggs Eggo Buttermilk Waffles–2 waffles
5. 360 mg Del Monte Peas And Carrots–½ cup (canned)
6. 70 mg C&W Ultimate Petite Mixed Vegetables–¾ cup (frozen)
7. 260 mg Tostitos Medium All Natural Salsa–2 tbsp
8. 1,190 mg Digiorno Four Cheese For One Traditional Crust Pizza–1 pizza
9. 770 mg Hot Pockets Frozen Food Ham and Cheese–1 piece
10. 820 mg Betty Crocker Lasagna Hamburger Helper–½ cup

## Answers to Activity #5:

Blueberries, cranberries, blackberries, raspberries, strawberries, oranges, grapefruits, tangerines, lemons, limes, broccoli, cabbage, brussel sprouts, eggs, wheat grass, spirulina, chlorella, barley grass, spinach, kale, Swiss chard, romaine lettuce, bok choy, collards, dried beans, edamame, fresh green beans, almonds, brazil nuts, pecans, walnuts, oatmeal, oat bran, olives, olive oil, wild salmon, tuna, trout, sardines, pumpkin, butternut squash, sweet potatoes, carrots, yams, dulse, hijiki, kombu, wakame, flaxseeds, pumpkin seeds, sunflower seeds, soybeans, soymilk, soy protein powder, green tea, white tea, black tea, oolong tea, tomatoes, turkey, barley, rye, wheat, yogurt, and kefir.

# PART III

# Beyond Food

We're staying in tonight.

# CHAPTER 7

# The Mental Game

---

## Love

Let's move beyond food and get into some heavy stuff, like why we over-eat. To understand why we overeat, we have to examine our relationship with food. Most of us believe we either have a good relationship with food or a bad relationship with food. While this may be true for many of us, it certainly doesn't cover the gamut of relationships out there.

Let's start with the positive. Let's assume you have a great relationship with food. Let's assume you overeat because you love food. If you overeat because you love food so much you can never leave it alone, you might want to hit your spouse up for some sex instead. I'm not saying sex is a replacement for food or vice versa, but at least it will keep you out of the kitchen for a while. If sex doesn't interest you, try charity work. You can get a lot of pleasure out of helping someone. The point is, if you overeat simply because you love food too much—and that's a legitimate problem— you should probably find a few other things to love.

Finding things you will love as much as food may not be easy, but dogs can come close. Finding things that will love you as unconditionally as food may not be easy either, but they are out there, and again, dogs come close. Stop and think here about some things you love, or would love to do, or would love to learn to do that don't involve eating. List some of those things here:

1. _____
2. _____
3. _____
4. _____
5. _____

Life is short. Use it wisely. Find things you love to do and spend some time doing them. Don't make food your only source of pleasure. You'll miss out.

## Love/Hate

Love is a terrific emotion, maybe the best there is, and in this troubled, violent world, we could all use more of it. But even things we love can hurt us, just like we can hurt things we love. If food, to you, is as much about pain as it is about love, you may be in a love/hate relationship with it. Love/hate relationships are, at best, confusing, and at worst, abusive. Signs that your relationship with food might be on the wrong track include:

- Candy bars insult you.

- Cookies stalk you.

- French fries keep calling you, even after you've asked them to leave you alone.

- Ice cream waits for you to come home, and then demands to know where you've been.

- Fried chicken batters you.

- Soda won't let you go anywhere without it.

- Donuts slap you around.

If your relationship with food is abusive, you'd be wise to spend less time with it and surround yourself with other activities that treat you better, like laundry. Look at that. Different relationship. Same solution. This time, list five things you've been meaning to do, but haven't found the time to do yet (no food involved).

1. _____
2. _____
3. _____
4. _____
5. _____

*Your* shelf life is limited too, you know. Don't waste it with things that treat you poorly.

## RELATIONSHIP EVALUATION QUESTION

Let's keep probing. Complete the following statement by circling all that apply.

I eat when I'm...

| | |
|---|---|
| hungry | awake |
| not hungry | at home |
| alone | at work |
| with others | at the mall |
| upset | at parties |
| tired | in the car |
| bored | on the go |
| frustrated | watching TV |
| lonely | doing something |
| stressed | not doing something |
| depressed | avoiding doing something |
| happy | doing nothing |

# Friends

If you circled *alone* or *lonely*, you may be in a Companion Relationship with food. Companion Relationships, in general, aren't bad, but they're best reserved for things we don't consume. That's because once they're gone, we miss them and seek them out again. Just like people mistakenly make drugs or alcohol their companion, Companion Relationships with food can sometimes go awry. Sugar and salt may not have the addictive qualities of drugs or alcohol, but they still keep up coming back for more.

By the way, the food industry, like the tobacco industry, like the alcohol industry, loves when we make their products our companion. Going to the movies alone? Not if you have candy and soda with you. If food is your number one companion, it's probably time to make some new friends.

# Rescuers

If you circled *upset, frustrated,* and the like, you may be in an Emotional Rescue Relationship with food. That is, you've come to depend on food to solve your problems and the emotions that go with them. As you learned way back in Chapter 1, advertisers want you to believe food has magic problem-solving qualities. As you've learned from your entire life, it doesn't.

I'm no life coach, although I hear they make a good living by asking people what they want to do, then telling them to go do it. All I can say is that if you're certain you overeat because you're depressed or stressed or down about something, you might as well figure out what that something is and try to fix it. Chances are your job and/or your relationship has something to do with it. If that's the case, do what you need to do to change or improve whatever the problem is. If that means a new job and a new relationship, I'm sorry for your boss and your partner, but hey, you aren't getting any younger. If you like your job and your relationship but you're still unhappy, maybe you're just difficult to please.

Either way, overeating doesn't solve anything. All overeating does is distract you so you don't have to deal with the difficult stuff. Then, before you know it, your pants don't fit either, and now you have two problems.

## Circus Seals

If you circled everything, you may be, like many Americans, in a Circus Seal Relationship with food, meaning you've been conditioned to behave a certain way, just like circus seals. For example, if you jump up to get a snack every time the commercials come on, you might think you've outsmarted the advertisers, but you would be wrong. Advertisers expect us to jump up during the commercials. Advertisers have trained us to jump up during the commercials. That's why they turn up the sound so loud, so we can hear them from the kitchen. And what have advertisers trained us to do?

**Advertisers have trained us to eat as a secondary activity.**

And not just at home. The training carries over to everything we do. We can't drive without a cup of coffee. We can't shop without a cookie. We can't sit through a game without a beer and a hot dog. Having a beer and a hot dog at the game is great fun, but it never stops there. First it's the beer and hot dog, then it's the peanuts and popcorn, then it's ice cream and cotton candy. The consumption never ends. If you're in a Circus Seal Relationship with food and you're trying to lose weight, you might want to go to more theater. You usually can't bring food in there.

## Controlling Ourselves

Whatever our relationship with food may be, controlling the habit to overeat is no easy task. That's why some of us head to the drugstore for help, where an assortment of pills and supplements await us. The big newcomer, Alli, which advertises itself as "the only FDA-approved weight loss product," works by "preventing the absorption of some of the fat you eat." Side effects, called "treatment effects" by the manufacturer on its website, include "gas with oily spotting, loose stools," and "more fre-quent stools that may be hard to control." So while it may be safe by FDA standards, it doesn't mean it's pleasant. To lessen the "treatment effects,"

the manufacturer suggests you "limit your fat intake in your meals to an average of 15 grams." Of course, if you limit your fat intake to an average of 15 grams per meal, you'll likely lose weight anyway, minus the gas, diarrhea, and cost of the pills.

If Alli is the only FDA-approved weight loss product, does that mean all those other over-the-counter weight loss pills and supplements aren't FDA approved? Pretty much. It's true that since 1994 there has been something in place called the Dietary Supplement Health and Education Act (DSHEA), but that act only requires the FDA to check out an over-the-counter diet drug when a new ingredient has been used. That means all those ingredients that were on the market before 1994 get to stay on the market, and are considered safe until proven otherwise, as in the people who take them start to drop dead. And under the DSHEA, it's up to the FDA to make a case against something before it can take it off the market. In other words, the companies that make and sell these products never have to prove anything to anyone. According to the FDA, except for the above-mentioned act:

There is no provision under any law or regulation that FDA enforces that requires a firm to disclose to FDA or consumers the information they have about the safety or purported benefits of their dietary supplement products.

What? What happened to "protecting the public health by assuring the safety, efficacy, and security of human and veterinary drugs, biological products, medical devices, our nation's food supply, cosmetics, and products that emit radiation"? I told you it was too much to saddle one agency with all that. The FDA even admits it on its website page, "Overview of Dietary Supplements."

The agency does not analyze dietary supplements before they are sold to consumers. The manufacturer is responsible for ensuring that the "Supplement Facts" label and ingredient list are accurate, that the dietary ingredients are safe, and that the content matches the amount declared on the label. FDA does not have resources to analyze dietary supplements sent to the agency by consumers who want to know their content. Instead, consumers may contact the manufacturer or a commercial laboratory for an analysis of the content.

You mean we're supposed to trust the people who make this stuff? That doesn't sound like a good idea. Listen, I don't doubt a mix of caffeine and laxatives will keep you moving and out of the kitchen, but is that really how you want to spend your day?

So how do we control ourselves without special effects, like pills and supplements? The same way we control toddlers—with discipline. Just for the record, I don't have kids, so I'm not an expert in this either, but I do have a lot of nieces and nephews. I can also draw from my own childhood experiences and suggest the following, unexhausted list of disciplinary actions:

- **No Dessert.** Just like you might send little Johnny to bed with no dessert, you might try cutting out sweets, treats, candy, chocolate, cookies, cakes, pastries, donuts, and soda. That still doesn't mean you can eat as much pasta and cheese as you want, but by cutting out sweets and treats you'll be eliminating a lot of high-fat, empty calories. Empty calories are like politicians—they do nothing for us. Does that mean you can never eat sweets again? No. But first you have to prove you can behave in front of them.

- **Wash Your Mouth Out with Soap.** I don't really think you should wash your mouth out with soap, but you might consider brushing your teeth and washing your mouth out with mouthwash. Brushing your teeth is a great way to signal to your mouth that you're done eating. For example, if you brush your teeth right after dinner instead of three hours later when you go to bed, you may have an easier time avoiding those late-night munchies. Plus you'll have nice fresh breath in case someone wants to kiss you.

- **Take a Time-out.** When I was a kid, if you misbehaved you got sent to your room. In the world of modern parenting, this is now called a "time-out." Time-outs are effective, parenting counselors say, because you remove the child from the problem instead of removing the problem from the child, which takes more time. The same strategy works when it comes to overeating. You will help yourself a lot by removing yourself from places where you find food, like the break room, the kitchen, and the buffet, for food, not surprisingly, is the number one stimulant of appetite.

- **Spank.** I don't think you should spank yourself either, but a gentle pat on the rear may remind you that your butt is too big. It seems to me when we overeat, we never think about that. We just think about our mouth. Our mouth wants more and we oblige. The joke is our mouth doesn't even get fat. However you do it, when you eat, try to remember that your mouth is just a small part of you, and the rest of your body shouldn't have to pay for its indulgences.

Maybe you don't agree. Maybe you think discipline is parochial and outdated. I think it's underrated and underused. We can thank lawyers for that. The result is a lot of cushy parenting, cushy schooling, cushy parents, and cushy kids. America is Pinocchio's Pleasure Island, only we aren't turning into donkeys, we're turning into pigs.

## Social Conformity

Beyond our relationship with food is our relationship with other people. Since, in general, most of us like to be part of the group, sometimes we overeat just because everybody else is overeating. It's as if we draw two conclusions:

1. That if everybody else is still eating, it must be okay to eat more, and

2. That if we don't keep eating like everybody else, no one will like us.

Both of these conclusions are false. Still, it helps to know how to handle these awkward situations. We can:

- Talk
- Listen
- Look around
- Watch other people eat
- Leave

Talking is probably our safest bet. Listening isn't bad either, but if everybody else at the table is still eating, all we hear is people chewing. At restaurants, it's fun to listen in on other people's conversations, but don't join in unless you plan to pick up their check too. It's also fun to look around at restaurants, but it's easy for other people to get the wrong idea, especially your date.

Keep in mind that talking does not mean complaining, nagging, or whining. If it's impossible for you to open your mouth without doing any of the above, you don't just need to change your eating habits, you need to change your attitude too.

The easiest way to change our attitude is to have some gratitude for the things we have, which is a lot more than most people on this planet. The short list includes food, running water, and electricity. Of course, we all have our down days, and sometimes even the most serious discussion can't be avoided, but it's best to have these in expensive restaurants where we're forced to behave and keep our voice at a reasonable level.

Overall, eating with other people should be a pleasant social experience, an occasion to relax, and a time to enjoy the company we're with. In general, conversations about politics, religion, sex, and money can spark more heated responses than conversations about movies, celebrities, books, and the weather. Sports can go either way. If all else fails, gossip. Whatever you decide to talk about, it's just as rude to hog the conversation as it is to hog the potato salad. Also, if while you're talking, people stop eating and begin to yawn, you may want to consider changing topics.

By the way, pleasant easygoing conversation isn't just for company, coworkers, and strangers. Your spouse is a person too. Perhaps if instead of always nagging them, you engaged them in some pleasant easygoing conversation, they might be inclined to treat you with the same courtesy they treat strangers.

Even if you eat alone regularly, your meal should still be a pleasant social experience, an occasion to relax, and a time to enjoy the company you're with. If you don't enjoy your own company, chances are others don't either, which may be part of the problem.

Whether alone or with others, you will probably always have to swat away suggestions to eat more. When alone, simply tell yourself, "That's enough," and then sit with that thought for a minute, so when you carry your plate back to the kitchen, you're clear on the plan. When other people tell you eat to more, just politely decline, as in:

"No thank you, I've had enough."

"I'm fine. Thanks. Everything was delicious."

"I'm full. Thank you. It was great."

These may, or may not, do the trick. In the beginning, other people will probably be suspicious and may, or may not, be supportive, so keep declining politely. What you don't want to do is get angry and blurt out "Why? So you can feel better about stuffing yourself?" Other responses to avoid include:

"Get off my back, fatso!"

"What are trying to do? Kill me!"

"Why? Cause tubby wants a friend?"

If you are constantly eating with people who elicit these kinds of angry responses from you, you don't just need to change your eating habits, you also need to change the company you keep, even if they are blood related.

## Creating Healthy Relationships

In a perfect world, we'd all have perfect relationships, but that would mean none of us have parents. No relationship is perfect. A relationship may look perfect to the outside world, but be assured you don't know the whole story. Even when you are right smack in the middle of the relationship, chances are you don't know the whole story.

Perfect relationships don't exist, except with dogs, and I'm sure Fido has his list of issues too. If your goal is to have perfect relationships, you're setting yourself up for disappointment.

**Perfect relationships aren't the goal. Healthy relationships are.**

Whether it's with food or your lover, here are some ways to make your relationships healthier:

- **Choose wisely.** When dating, single people are better than married people. When eating, single portions are better than double portions.

- **Don't misbehave away from home.** Whether it's your sexy colleague or a chocolate cream pie, if you bring either of them up to your hotel room, things may get out of hand.

- **Don't go to bed angry or stuffed.** You will ruin a good night's sleep. And don't even talk about sex.

- Speaking of sex, **don't confuse sex with food**, or food with love, or love with sex, or food with your partner.

- **Know that every relationship has its ups and downs.** Just as you don't always like your partner, you won't always like having to eat less. For what it's worth, no one likes you all the time either, and they deal with it.

- **Don't be boring.** Whether it's your love life or food: if it's in a rut, then find ways to spice it up.

- **Let stuff go.** That means don't bring stuff up that happened a year ago. And if you ate too much last night, get over it and get back on track.

- **Don't expect fairy tales.** There is no Prince Charming. There is no quick weight-loss miracle either.

Take responsibility. Not everything is your partner's fault. Not everything is society's fault. Not everything is food's fault. Some of it is your fault.

## Being Kind

At the heart of all worthwhile relationships is kindness. Whatever your relationship with food, be kind to yourself. Don't keep ice cream in the house if it taunts you. Don't eat with people who make you so uncomfortable you have to stuff yourself to get through the meal. Don't fill your cupboards with cookies if you love cookies so much you can't deny them, then you hate yourself for eating them. Don't just find friendship, love, and companionship in food. Find friendship, love, and companionship. Food is a part of life. It's not all there is to it.

**Stop connecting every dot to food.**

## Let's Sum It Up

- Happy or sad, if you eat too much, you will gain weight.

- If you want to be adored, get a dog.

- Some pills cause cramps and diarrhea.

- The only problem food solves is hunger.

- Discipline isn't just for children.

- Other people aren't always that helpful.

- Sometimes you have to go it on your own.

# Reprogramming Activities

### Activity #1–Distract Yourself Kindly

Learning to control yourself around food might take some time, so if it helps, distract yourself until you get a little better at it. This is harder than it sounds because, as a culture, we've been brainwashed to use food as a distraction. That means we need a distraction for our distraction. In the modern world, that's usually shopping. But there are lots of other things you can do that are easier on your budget.

| | |
|---|---|
| Call someone. | Clean something. |
| Help someone. | Read something. |
| Visit someone. | Play something. |

You get the idea.

## Activity #2—Levels of Alert

To help better handle those times when you are more in danger of overeating (emotionally or otherwise), I've devised the following advisory system, a color-coded threat level thing, just like the professionals use and from whom I borrowed heavily. I'm sure the folks at Homeland Security won't mind, and they may even be flattered to know their system has found new legs. Just like the government's system, our system has five threat levels, each with its very own color. From low to high risk, the threat levels and colors are:

### OVEREATING ADVISORY SYSTEM

| | | |
|---|---|---|
| 1. | Green | Low risk of eating too much |
| 2. | Blue | Guarded risk of eating too much |
| 3. | Yellow | Elevated risk of eating too much |
| 4. | Orange | High risk of eating too much |
| 5. | Red | Severe risk of eating too much |

For example, Thanksgiving is Threat Level Red. On Thanksgiving, most of us have a severe risk of eating too much. Go ahead and list below the times when and the types of situations where you eat too much. Maybe it's when you walk in the door after work, maybe it's when you watch TV at night, maybe it's when you're out to eat. If it's all day long—don't be embarrassed—just realize you're going to be at Threat Level Red for a while. After you've listed your problem times and situations, give each of those times or situations your own personal threat level assessment.

1. _____ Threat Level _____

2. _____ Threat Level _____

3. _____ Threat Level _____

4. _____ Threat Level _____

5. _____ Threat Level _____

If you're as overweight as most of the country is, you'll probably be at Threat Level Orange most of the time, except when you sleep and then you can go down to Yellow. Be prepared for these high-risk situations. Understand when you are more vulnerable to overeating and be ready to fight back. At every level of elevated risk, remember to:

- **Be vigilant.** Don't eat with your eyes closed.

- **Take notice of your surroundings.** If you're seated next to the mashed potatoes, be aware that an attack could occur at any moment. Feel free to pass the mashed potatoes to the other end of the table before the situation escalates out of control.

- **If necessary, establish a No-Eat list.** For example, when you go to a restaurant, consider putting bread on your No-Eat list for the evening. If you can't resist the basket just sitting there, hand it to your waiter and say something pleasant like, "Please take this in the back for questioning."

## Activity #3—Table Manners

Just about all of us could work on our table manners. At your next meal, turn off the TV, put away the magazine, and consider the following suggestions:

- **Chew.** Some say the easiest way to control our weight is to chew more, so next time you sit down, really give it a go. Not only will your system have an easier time digesting what you've eaten, your brain receptors will have more time to register it too. Your brain receptors don't work nearly as fast as your mouth does. Why not? Who knows? Maybe they have a lot of paperwork to fill out. Whatever the reason, those brain receptors take about 20 minutes to get the message from your stomach that you've had enough to eat, so slow down. If there's anything you should know by now, it's that you can't rush the system. While you chew, think about why we eat so fast in this country. Are we always in a hurry? Or just in the habit of eating fast?

- **Swallow.** After you chew, swallow. I know you're proud of your quick hand/mouth reflex, but your mouth isn't a conveyor belt. Put something in your mouth, taste it, chew it, and swallow it before you shove another mouthful in. Not only will you suffer less indigestion, but you'll put on a much nicer show for the person sitting across from you.

- **Put your utensil down.** A fork is not an appendage. You can actually release your fork and not lose any blood, so while you're chewing and swallowing, put your utensil down. Don't worry. You won't lose it. It'll still be there when you're ready for your next bite. Then, before you pick it up again, take a breath or a sip of water. I know you've got other things to do, like get to dessert, but don't sprint through your meals. If nothing else, you'll burp less.

- **At some point, stop eating.** If you stop eating and feel comfortably satisfied, but not full, that's a good sign. If you stop eating and feel slightly embarrassed, and ready to burst, that's a bad sign. If you stop eating so you can look for your pants button, which has shot across the room, that's not a good sign either. The goal is to get up from the table and still be able to function. The goal is not to fall off your chair and roll to the couch. If incentives help, keep in mind it's hard to make sexy on a full stomach. Don't you want to at least keep your options open?

## Activity #4—Need vs. Want

*Needing* food and *wanting* food are two different things. To understand which desire it is you're feeding when you eat, use my handy Hunger Scale. Level 1 is Extreme Hunger. Level 10 is Gluttony. If you're somewhere between Level 1 and Level 3, it's time to eat; you need some food. If every time you eat, you eat to Level 7 or above—it's time to stop; you need a muzzle.

### NEED VS. WANT HUNGER SCALE

1. Get the gurney. I can't get up.

2. I'm so hungry I can't remember where I hid the cookies.

3. My stomach is growling louder than my wife.

4. Where's the buffet?

5. Nothing hits the spot like BBQ ribs.

6. You know what I like after ribs? Spaghetti.

7. Man, I'm full. Hey, look! They just brought out more shrimp!

8. It's a good thing I wore my sweat pants or I wouldn't have room for dessert.

9. I'm so stuffed I can't eat another bite. I'll just put this cookie in my purse.

10. Get the gurney. I can't get up.

Speaking of buffets, understand that it's practically impossible not to overeat at them. First, you're trying to get your money's worth. Second, there's all that food. Why tempt yourself? If you're having problems with your spouse, do you call your ex-lover and go to the Erotic Expo? I hope not.

## Activity #5—Gratitude List

Gratitude is powerful. Unfortunately, in this country, we're taught not to have it. That way we're never satisfied and we keep consuming.

Chances are your life is filled with plenty of things for which you should be grateful. List some of those things here. If you can, try not to include things you just bought.

_____

_____

_____

_____

_____

_____

Use as many extra pieces of paper as you need, then tape it somewhere where you'll see it often. If you tape it somewhere where your spouse will see it too, be sure he or she is at the top of the list. That's just good manners.

## Activity #6—How's Your Social Circle?

We all pick friends who share similar interests, even if those interests aren't the best for us. What kinds of interests do you share with your friends? What kinds of things do you do when you spend time together?

_____

_____

_____

_____

_____

_____

What do you think? Do you need some new interests? Or do you need some new friends?

## Activity #7–Discipline

What's happened to supposedly core American values like hard work, honesty, and discipline? Do we believe in them anymore? Are they out-dated, or just no fun? Is coming out ahead better than coming out behind, regardless of how you do it? What three values do you value the most?

1. _____

2. _____

3. _____

Do you practice these values or just admire them from afar? Anything there you can use to help control yourself?

I think it makes your butt look smaller.

# CHAPTER 8

# Modern Bodies

———

## The Body

Let's move on to the body. If you're very overweight, you probably don't take care of your body as well as you could. Chances are you don't even like it. Hardly anybody likes his or her body these days. We can thank the media for that too.

By the media, I mean television, billboards, magazines, the Internet, and anywhere else you see Victoria's Secret models. It's not just Victoria's Secret, obviously, but at the moment I can't think of anybody else who airs a primetime panty show on network television.

In all fairness, if I were selling brown paper bags, I'd hire Victoria's Secret models to wear them, then I'd air a primetime brown paper bag show on network television and watch sales go through the roof. Let's face it: some people just look good in anything. When models don't look good in something, there are usually a slew of stylists around who can help. What stylists can't fix, Photoshop can. That's why it's fun to flip through the tabloids. You can always count on *National Enquirer* to snap an unbecoming shot of some celebrity's cellulite.

Fashion doesn't help either, because so many of us buy whatever a Victoria's Secret model is wearing, and then seem surprised when it doesn't do for us whatever it did for them. Just remember that fashion, like food, is business. It has to sell to make money. If you bought a pair of skinny jeans one season because they were the trend, you can be sure they won't be the trend next season.

Women especially go around looking ridiculous wearing the latest fashion when it does nothing to compliment their figures. Men don't make quite the same mistake, but they can look just as ridiculous in their shorts with their big bare belly hanging out for everyone to see.

**Male or female, whatever your body type, there is something you can wear to flatter it. Skinny jeans probably aren't it.**

## Your Body Image

People who don't like their bodies often think they will like them better once they lose some weight. This is probably true, but not always, which is why most TV extreme makeovers include some kind of implant. Maybe you will like your body better after you lose some weight, or maybe you will just find something else that's wrong with it (women especially have been brainwashed to do this).

Let's see where your body image is with my short, insightful Body Image Quiz.

### A SHORT, INSIGHTFUL BODY IMAGE QUIZ

1. When people compliment my appearance,
   I'm pretty sure they want something.      True     False

2. If there were a return counter for bodies, I'd get
   in line and demand to speak to the manager.     True     False

3. Chairs have nicer legs than I do.      True     False

4. I prefer to have sex in the dark.      True     False

5. I prefer to exercise in the dark.      True     False

6. I prefer to weigh myself in the dark.      True     False

7. At parties, I hide behind the ice sculpture.      True     False

8. If someone invites me to the beach, I usually come down with a quick case of smallpox.     True     False

9. I can't wait until I'm old and people stop staring at me.     True     False

If you answered more True than False, you may have a negative body image. Having a negative body image isn't necessarily life-threatening, but it can put a damper on fun. In some cases, very negative body images can lead to distorted body images, which can lead to dangerous eating disorders, which can lead to death, like collapsing from heart failure.

On the other hand, overly positive body images can also lead to distorted body images, which can also lead to dangerous eating habits, which can also lead to death, like exploding from satisfaction.

**You can love yourself fat and use that as an excuse to overeat just as easily as you can hate yourself fat and use that as your excuse to overeat.**

Does that mean body image is irrelevant? No. But it's not as reliable as the scale.

More important than a positive or a negative body image is a *healthy* body image, with more emphasis on the "healthy" and less emphasis on the "image." If you have a positive body image but you sit around and eat all day, it's probably time to stop patting yourself on the back and eat less. If you have a negative body image and you sit around and eat all day, it's probably time to stop picking on yourself and eat less. Either way, it's probably time to eat less.

# What Size You Come In

In all fairness, it's not your body's fault it is the way it is. It's yours. And your parents: By your parents, I mean that random genetic code you got. I know your parents have a lot more to answer for than that, but you can't spend your whole life blaming them for everything. How they ate and how they took care of themselves when you were growing up may have something to do with how you've eaten and how you've taken care of yourself over the years, but you've contributed to that mess too. Besides, as an adult, it's time to stop blaming everybody else for your life and take your wheel. You can change course. What you can't change is your genetic code and the basic body type it gave you.

People who need to lose weight love to talk about body type. This is what we call "changing the subject." Usually, the conversation goes something like this:

> **Lisa:  Those pants need to be let out.**
>
> **George:  How about those Knicks?**

It's true that bodies come in different shapes and sizes, and understanding your shape and size does have some utility, but it's no excuse for your pants not fitting anymore. Still, most of us spend a lot of time thinking about our size and shape, so let's address them as part of our reprogramming process.

Human bodies, historically, come in three sizes: small, medium and large. This size, often referred to as body frame, is determined by the size of your wrist in relation to your height. For example, you can be short with a large frame or tall with a small frame. To find out what size you are, try any or all of the following tests.

## THE FIRST WRIST TEST

To conduct the first wrist test, simply wrap your right index finger and thumb around the smallest part of your left wrist. If your finger and thumb touch, congratulations, you are medium framed. If they don't touch, congratulations, you are large framed. And if they overlap, congratulations, you are small framed.

## THE SECOND WRIST TEST

To conduct the second wrist test, measure your wrist at its smallest part and see where that measurement falls according to the following chart:

| WOMEN | | | |
|---|---|---|---|
| Height | Small | Medium | Large |
| Under 5'2" | < 5.5" | 5.5 - 5.75" | > 5.75" |
| 5'2"-5'5" | < 6.00" | 6.00 - 6.25" | > 6.25" |
| Over 5'5" | < 6.25" | 6.25 - 6.5" | > 6.5" |
| MEN | | | |
| Height | Small | Medium | Large |
| Over 5'5" | 5.5 - 6.5" | 6-5 - 7.5" | > 7.5" |

Are the wrist tests perfect? What test is? The wrist tests are particularly flawed if you're overweight and you carry the extra weight in your wrists. Maybe at your current weight you're large framed, but if you lost some weight, you might be medium framed. In other words, how can you possibly know what size your frame is under all that fat? The other reason the wrist tests are flawed is because it's entirely possible for you to have very tiny wrists and an extra large body, just like a tyrannosaur.

## THE ELBOW TEST

To conduct the elbow test, measure the breadth of your elbow. What's the breadth of your elbow? Apparently, it's the distance between the two prominent bones of your elbow joint. Some say this test is more accurate than the wrist tests, probably because it's hard to carry extra fat in your elbow joint. Or maybe it's just harder to disprove because the measurement is so hard to take. If you'd like to try, hold your arm out, then lift your forearm up to the ceiling with your hand facing in. From this position, using your other hand, feel for your elbow joint and then measure straight across. How? Exactly. Your elbow is in the way. If you get an accurate reading, here's what you do with it when you're done.

|            | WOMEN |
| :---: | :---: |
| **Medium Body Frame** | |
| Height | Elbow breadth (inches) |
| 4'10"-4'11" | 2¼ – 2½ |
| 5'0" -5'3" | 2¼ – 2½ |
| 5'4" -5'7" | 2⅜ – 2⅝ |
| 5'8" -5'11" | 2⅜ – 2⅝ |
| 6'0" | 2½ – 2¾ |
| | MEN |
| **Medium Body Frame** | |
| Height | Elbow breadth (inches) |
| 5'2"-5'3" | 2½ – 2⅞ |
| 5'4"-5'7" | 2⅝ – 1⅞ |
| 5'8"-5'11" | 2¾ – 3 |
| 6'0"-6'3" | 2¾ – 3⅛ |

If your measurement is smaller than the one listed here for your height, congratulations, you are small framed. If it's larger, congratulations, you are large framed.

What do you do if you get varying results from each test? If you're like most overweight people, you will probably pick the larger size. Practically everyone does. Practically everyone who needs to lose weight is large framed. Just ask them. Whatever your frame size, if you have rolls around your waist, extra chins, or lumpy legs, you probably could stand to lose a few pounds. In other words, frame size is no excuse not to control yourself.

## Body Types

Just as there are different frame sizes, there are also different body shapes. In the 1940s, U.S. psychiatrist Dr. William Sheldon gave us endomorphs, mesomorphs and ectomorphs. Based on the three embryonic germ layers (the three different layers of tissue in a fertilized egg), Dr. Sheldon believed his classification system could not only determine one's tendency to gain weight or lose weight, but also one's whole personality. For example:

- **Endomorphs** (inner germ "endo" from which the gastrointestinal tract develops) are round, friendly people who have a tendency to gain weight easily, and like to sit in recliners.

  Famous endomorphs: the Pillsbury Dough Boy, Bob of Bob's Big Boy, Homer Simpson.

- **Mesomorphs** (middle germ layer "meso" from which muscles and bone develop) are muscular, athletic people who have a tendency to bully others, and like to go into real estate.

  Famous mesomorphs: Rambo, The Terminator, most Superheros.

- **Ectomorphs** (outer germ "ecto" from which the skin and sense organs develop) are tall, thin, awkward people who have a tendency to bump their head on things, and like to go to the library.

  Famous ectomorphs: Ichabod Crane, Jack Skellington (king of Halloweentown).

Of course, there's a lot of crossover too, which happens when endos have sex with mesos, or mesos with ectos, or rock stars with supermodels.

There's also the popular Body as Fruit Classification System (my name for it). For example, some of us are round like apples, while others of us are hippy like pears. To understand what kind of body type you have, answer the following question:

**I tend to carry extra weight in my _____.**

If you tend to carry extra weight in your middle, congratulations, you're an apple. If you carry it in your hips, congratulations, you're a pear. If you have a difficult time narrowing in on one part of your body where the fat pools, congratulations, you're a watermelon.

Again, the current government position is that overweight apple types who carry fat in the middle, around all those important organs, are more at risk for health complications than overweight pear types who carry extra weight in the lower body (around all those important organs, wink, wink). But not everyone's on board. New studies are finding that, regardless of our body type, carrying fat in the liver is what increases our risk for disease. What causes fatty liver disease? Well, among other things, obesity. So how do you slim down your liver? The same way you slim down your belly—by losing excess weight.

Perhaps the most important thing we can take away for all of this is that regardless of our size or shape, there's no excuse for not fitting into our pants anymore.

**We cannot change our basic body type, but we can change the condition it's in.**

And we should probably get to it. Yes, we live longer, work smarter, and communicate faster these days, but we also sit too much, eat too much, and keep getting rounder. In fact, one expert says we're getting so round as a species that an evolutionary shift in the human body is occurring: we're slowly turning into Cinnabons. And it's not just Americans either. It's happening in industrialized countries everywhere. You think Global Warming is bad? Wait until you see what Global Fattening does to the species. Maybe the two are even linked.

Linking Global Warming and Global Fattening isn't as ridiculous as it sounds. According to Paul Higgins of the American Association for the Advancement of Science, Americans could cut carbon emissions by 64 million tons if they would cut their driving by thirty minutes a day and use some other way, like walking or biking, to get where they're going. Along the way, Americans would lose 3 billion pounds of fat.

I haven't checked the math on it yet, and the plan isn't without its flaws, mainly that none of us would get to work on time, but there's something to be said for spending less time in the car.

# The Business of Exercise

*Lack of activity destroys the good condition of every human being, while movement and methodical physical exercise save it and preserve it.*

—PLATO

Or your mother used to say,

*Get up!*

—YOUR MOTHER

That's right. We need to get up and get some exercise. That's what everybody tells us, starting with our doctor and ending with the food industry. Why does the food industry want us to get some exercise? Because it wants us to believe the problem isn't what or how much we eat, but how little we exercise. That's so we can keep eating as much as we do. You can eat anything you want as you long as exercise enough, it tells us. Maybe, if you're a long distance runner. Running guru James Fixx was pretty thin when he dropped dead of a heart attack.

In other words, excessive exercise isn't any more a solution than excessive dieting. Yes, we can all benefit from some sort of physical activity, but we don't all have to train for the Ironman triathlon to get it. For those of you who want to train for the Ironman triathlon: good for you. The rest of us can benefit just dandy with something more moderate. The problem with moderation is it doesn't sell. The fitness industry is hardly the size of the diet industry, but it'd love to sell you an expensive gym membership, some fancy fitness clothes, and a $150 pair of shoes.

Why does the medical industry want us to get some serious exercise? They say it's for our health, but who do you have to go see when you get hurt? Am I saying the medical industry conspires with the exercise industry? No. I'm just saying the medical industry, like the fitness industry, like the food industry, is in the business of making money. Our excesses, from overeating to over exercising, drive them all.

190

## Walk It Off

The easiest way for all of us to get the physical activity we need is to simply start walking. In fact, according to experts from UC Berkeley, a 200-pound person who starts walking a mile and a half a day will lose about 14 pounds a year, without even changing how many calories he or she consumes.

Do you know how long it takes to walk a mile and a half? Thirty minutes. That means you can go out the door, walk for fifteen minutes in one direction, turn around, and walk back, and if you do that every day for a year, at the end of the year, you'll be about 14 pounds lighter. And if you don't have time to take one 30-minute walk, you can take three ten-minute walks and get pretty much the same benefit.

Nothing beats walking. Hippocrates, the great ancient Greek physician, also known as the "Father of medicine," knew it way back in the Age of Pericles, a couple hundreds years before the birth of Christ. Did he go down in history saying, "Here, take this new the pharmaceutical we're pushing"? No, he went down in history saying,

*Walking is the best medicine.*

—HIPPOCRATES

Not just doctors, but philosophers knew it too. The Great Dane of Western Philosophy, Soren Kierkegaard said,

*Above all, do not lose your desire to walk. Every day I walk myself into a state of well-being and walk away from every illness. I have walked myself into my best thoughts, and I know of no thought so burdensome that one cannot walk away from it.*

—SOREN KIERKEGAARD

Thomas Jefferson, great American president and main author of the Declaration of Independence agreed.

*Of all exercises walking is the best.*

—THOMAS JEFFERSON

I'll add my own name to that list of great thinkers by saying,

*There's nothing like a walk to get a break from your family.*

—LISA PEDACE

I've been walking for twenty years and all of my relationships have been better for it.

# How Much Physical Activity We Need

According to the CDC, all of us need 30 minutes of moderate-intensity aerobic activity, like walking, at least five times a week. For even greater health benefits, they recommend 300 minutes a week (that's a 45 minute walk, seven days a week). Other groups, like the non-profit think tank, the Institute of Medicine of the National Academies, would like to see us get 60 minutes of moderate-intensity activity each day. That can seem like a lot of time, but it's a lot less than most of spend watching television, so chances are we all have time for it. All each of us has to do is decide to make it a priority.

Making something a priority is easier than you think and usually involves some kind of list making, which is especially useful as we age and can't remember half the things we're supposed to be doing. It may very well be that you have every intention to get some physical activity, but because you never write it down, you simply forget and have a sandwich.

So let's make a list. I'll fill in the first few just to get you started.

**Priority List for _____ (fill in today's date)**

1. 30-60 minutes of some kind of physical activity.
2. Say something nice to my partner.
3. Encourage my kid. (If you don't have a kid, encourage somebody.)
4. Lotion.
5. _____
6. _____
7. _____
8. _____

You can use this list over and over, or you can make a new one. Just remember to include those 30-60 minutes of physical activity each day. If it helps, schedule it as recess. Recess is defined as "a break period, typically outdoors, for children." You know what a break period is, typically outdoors, for adults? A cigarette.

# The Benefits of Physical Activity

However you decide to get it, the benefits of some exercise, which include better moods and better metabolism, far outweigh the benefits of no exercise, which include not having to shower as much and less laundry. Let's look at what they tell us those benefits are:

- **Better metabolism.** Metabolism, which is sort of our body's gas mileage, refers to how efficiently our body burns calories. Surprisingly, if you're overweight, your metabolism may already be working in high gear. That's because it's trying to move a Mack truck. However, once you begin to lose some weight, your metabolism can actually slow down because now you are a Mack truck without a big trailer behind you. That change in load can cause your metabolism to slow down. That's why people who lose weight can often plateau after a gangbuster start. Regular physical activity is what keeps the motor revving.

- **Better moods.** In general, regular physical activity makes us happier and less stressed. How this works isn't exactly clear, but scientists think it's because it wakes up some feel-good neurotransmitters in the brain, like serotonin and norepinephrine. They're up there sleeping half the time because nobody ever comes to check on them. Regular physical activity also stimulates the production of endorphins. Endorphins are the green M&Ms of neuro-transmitters, firing off every time we reach orgasm. But we get these relaxing, feel better, natural highs from physical activity too. If that doesn't inspire you to get up, what will?

- **Better sleep.** People who get regular physical activity generally fall asleep faster and sleep more soundly than people who sit around all day. They may also have fewer weight issues. What does sleeping better have to do with our weight? It turns out that people who sleep more are less likely to be obese. No one knows for sure yet why this is so, but a couple of theories exist. One is what I call the "Caveman in Summer" theory. It's based on the idea that Oogg will gain weight in the summer when the nights are shorter and food is more available to prepare him for the cold winter when the nights are longer and the Dino-Burger joint is closed. So if you're never getting enough sleep, your body may always be in the "Caveman in Summer" mode. Another possibility is that certain hormones may get out of whack when we don't sleep enough. Some studies suggest that leptin, a hormone that has something to do with appetite control, drops with too little sleep, while ghrelin, a hormone that has something to do with appetite stimulation, increases. And of course it may just be that we eat more 'cause we're up longer. Whatever it is, sleep is good for us and physical activity can improve the quality of it.

- **Better sex and health.** (I threw those in together because the concept of better health on its own hardly gets anybody excited anymore.) Here's how it works. Regular physical exercise gets the oxygen and the blood pumping. According the CDC, that can help battle certain chronic diseases, like heart disease, high blood pressure, and diabetes. Come to think of it, that's how the better sex thing works too. Regular physical exercise gets the oxygen and blood pumping!

Of course, if you want better moods, better sleep, and better sex, you could just take an antidepressant, a sleeping pill, and an erectile dysfunction pill. Scientists haven't quite figured out the better metabolism pill, so doctors aren't prescribing them yet, but that doesn't mean you can't buy some fat-burning magic dust over the counter at your local drugstore.

## Having Fun

In addition to some moderate physical activity, like walking, we could all benefit from a little more play. This very idea of more play is behind the advertising campaign trying to sell us the virtual game player, Wii Fit, for our TV. The commercial shows one person participating and exercising on the Wii Fit Balance Board, and three people on the couch watching (with big smiles, of course). I suppose it's better than all four people sitting on the couch watching, but only by one-fourth. To use the Wii Fit, you need buy the Wii console, the Wii Fit Balance Board, and additional games. Having never tried Wii Fit anything, I have no opinion on how well it works. I have tried Wii bowling, however, and it hardly resembles a trip to the bowling alley. Of course, not everyone can make it to the bowling alley, which is why, I suppose, Wii bowling has become a big hit in retirement homes where, according to Wikipedia, senior residents are forming their own Wii bowling leagues and having a blast. In other words, there's plenty of time to play virtual sports when we're almost dead. For now, shouldn't the rest of us be doing the real thing while we still can?

And isn't anyone else troubled by the fact that we're allowing future generations to be brainwashed to do everything in front of some kind of screen every minute of the day? (Stop and think here.)

The point here is that it would be nice if you played with your family somewhere besides in front of the TV.

## How Many Calories You'll Burn

If you read magazines, you've probably seen those ridiculous articles that try to encourage us to get some physical activity by telling us how many calories we'll burn an hour doing some particular thing, like having sex. For example, someone who weighs 200 pounds can burn 384 calories an hour having sex. Dandy. Do you know how many calories that person will burn having sex for 3 minutes? 19. That's it. That's a stalk of celery. So that great lovemaking session with your sweetheart gets you a stalk of celery. Like you need another reason to resent your spouse.

I'm not saying to skip the 3-minute fireworks sessions with your loved one. I'm just saying, don't focus on how many calories you're burning. You're not negotiating for a plate of mac and cheese. Besides, nobody ever gets the math right. Everybody always overestimates how many calories they burn and underestimates how many calories they eat.

> **Getting regular physical activity is not about how many calories you'll burn so you can eat more. Getting regular physical activity is about using your body every day so you can enjoy better health.**

In other words, you still have to eat less. You have to eat less and get some physical activity at the same time.

## Staying Motivated

Staying motivated to get some regular physical activity can take some getting used to, but like every part of a healthier lifestyle, it's a habit you can develop. If it helps, get other people involved. They're probably dying to get out the house too. Whether you take a walk with a friend or throw the ball around with your kids, it's never too late to incorporate some kind of daily activity into your life. Before you know it, you'll be in some box or urn, underground or on some mantel, stuck there for good, never able to stretch out again. Enjoy moving while you can.

*Money is the most envied, but the least enjoyed.*
*Health is the most enjoyed, but the least envied.*
—CHARLES CALEB COLTON

*Nothing beats being young.*
—LISA PEDACE

# Let's Sum It Up

- Frame size is important to know, but only if you need to frame something.

- People are like fruit. Some are sweet. Some are bitter. Some are bruised.

- There is no return counter for life.

- Having a positive body image doesn't mean you look good in tight clothes.

- Good health involves getting up.

- No one is too old to be physically active or pay taxes, not in that order.

- God designed the human body to move, not to sit. He didn't create a chair from Adam's rib; he created a dance partner.

- Walking isn't just for postmen.

## Reprogramming Activities

### Activity #1-What's Your Shape?

How would you describe your shape? These are not the personals, so go ahead and be honest. Circle all that apply. I've even included some blanks for you to fill in, in case you have some defining body part I didn't include:

| | |
|---|---|
| endomorph | ecto-mesomorph |
| mesomorph | endo-mesomorph |
| ectomorph | apple |
| meso-endomorph | pear |
| ecto-endomorph | watermelon |

| | |
|---|---|
| banana | thick legs |
| kiwi | thin legs |
| ruler | medium legs |
| funnel | wide chest |
| protractor | small chest |
| inverted protractor | medium chest |
| petite | flat chest |
| hourglass | hot sexy mama chest |
| gourd | narrow shoulders |
| scissors | broad shoulders |
| peanut | rounded shoulders |
| globe | muscular shoulders |
| short legs | _____ |
| long legs | _____ |

I'm sort of a pear-shaped mesomorph with broad shoulders, a long body, and short legs. How does this information help me? Well, I know I'll never be a Rockette. I also know that if I wear cropped pants, I look like an Oompa-Loompa. Go ahead and write in whatever you are:

**I'm sort of a** _____.

Now check one of the following boxes:

☐ That's okay with me.
☐ It ain't perfect, but it runs.
☐ You get what you pay for.

I hope you checked all three. Understanding and accepting our body size and type is a big part of the reprogramming process. In other words, we can suck the fat out of a walrus. That doesn't make it a dolphin. If you're an apple, you will always be an apple, but you don't have to be the fattest apple on the block.

## Activity #2—Making Peace with Your Body

Make peace with your body. List five things you like about it.

1. _____

2. _____

3. _____

4. _____

5. _____

Next time you start nitpicking about some part of your body, focus on one of the above instead.

## Activity #3—Body Part Game

There are 10 human body parts that are only 3 letters long. List them. As you run through the different parts of your body, stop and think about how valuable each part of your body is and how sorry you would be not to have that part. Think about how you should revere each part by taking the best care of it you possibly can. The correct answers are at the end of the chapter.

_____   _____   _____   _____   _____

_____   _____   _____   _____   _____

## Activity #4—Go Green

Why not give it a go? See if you can cut your driving by 30 minutes a day, or even 30 minutes a week. Maybe that means you skip that weekend trip to the mall, but so what? You'll not only cut back on emissions, you'll cut back on spending too.

## Activity #5—Fitness Infomercials

Whether it's for your abs or your inner thighs, infomercials selling at-home workout equipment abound. Next time you see one, pay attention to some of the claims being made. Quick results? The body you always wanted? Results not typical? You don't need to write anything down this time. In fact, why don't you get up and do some stretches instead? Look at that: quick results, without even taking your credit card out.

## Activity #6—Take a Walk, Baby!

Why not incorporate some regular walking into your life? I know some people find the idea of a walk boring, but like anything, it's all in the approach. To find out which approach might work for you, let's take another short quiz.

### WALKING STYLE QUIZ

1. Mention Bears and Cougars and I think of...
   a. sports jerseys
   b. animals
   c. my neighbors

2. In my spare time I like to...
   a. compare prices
   b. bird watch
   c. eavesdrop on my neighbors

3. I love to look at...
   a. catalogs
   b. the sunrise
   c. my neighbors' mail

4. When it comes to information, I'm up on...
   a. the newest products
   b. whatever's in bloom
   c. my neighbors' schedules

5. Nothing piques my interest like…

    a. the latest trends
    b. the changing seasons
    c. my neighbors' sex lives

If you answered mostly A, you're probably an informed consumer. Take an Information Walk. Check out homes for sale in your neighborhood. See what new cars are on the road. What's popular in home improvement this year? Or head to a mall and see what's new for the season. (Bring your ID. Leave your charge cards at home.)

If you answered mostly B, you're probably an earthy person who loves to experience the natural world around you. Take a Nature Walk. What season is it? What signs of the season are out there? How are the trees changing? What kinds of flowers do you see? What kinds of insects are you stepping on?

If you answered mostly C, you're probably a curious person who loves to observe others. Take a Neighborhood Walk and be your own Neighborhood Watch patrol person.

Shoot for at least thirty minutes every day. That's just 15 minutes in one direction and fifteen minutes back. If that's more than you're ready for, go for ten minutes, build up to twenty and so on. When you're finished, check all that apply:

☐   I walked for 30 minutes!
☐   It wasn't as hard as I thought.
☐   I feel energized.
☐   I think my neighbor is having an affair.

*Answers to Activity #3*

Eye, hip, arm, leg, ear, toe, jaw, rib, lip, gum.

I just started walking my own and before I knew it, I was in business.

# CHAPTER 9

# Keeping It Up

## Getting in the Habit

Like I said from the get-go, reprogramming ourselves is as easy as changing some of our habits, but staying committed to these new and better habits takes some effort. First we have to fight off messages from the media. Then we have to fight off messages from our brain.

Fighting off messages from the media is sometimes as simple as turning off our televisions, radios, and computers (come on, there's not *that* much news). Fighting off messages from our brain is a little more complicated because, unfortunately, we can never turn off our head. I say unfortunately because I think we would all enjoy a break from ourselves once in a while. Even when we're trying our hardest to do what's best for us, our brain can sometimes get in the way. I call this the "I'm Gonna Be the Boss Somewhere" syndrome.

To help you understand the "I'm Gonna Be the Boss Somewhere" syndrome, think of your brain as an out-of-control child who wants what it wants, when it wants it, and never wants to have to do anything extra to get it. Of course, the whole brain isn't like this, just the part that's in control. Freud referred to this part of the brain as the Id. Also up there in the brain with the Id, but cowering in the corner, are the Ego, and the Superego. Some modern psychiatrists refer to these three parts of brain as the Child, the Adult, and the Parent. Others call them Larry, Curly, and Moe. Whatever you call them, they're all up there, battling things out, and when it comes to how we eat and how well we take care of our body, our out-of-control child usually wins. Why? Because our out-of-control child doesn't care.

If you ever had your own tree house, you probably have already experienced the "I'm Gonna Be the Boss Somewhere" syndrome, which works like this: We get to make all the rules. As an adult, we know the outside world doesn't work like this, and once we're married, neither does our home.

> **As an adult, the only thing we get to make all the rules about is our body and how we take care of it.**

Want to rebel? Have a cookie. Want a reward? Have a cookie. Want a cookie? Have a cookie. For some reason, the rest of the brain just rolls over and agrees. Why? How should I know? I just made the syndrome up. My guess is the rest of the brain probably agrees: We should get to be the boss somewhere. Or maybe the rest of the brain is too tired to resist. Either way, the body complies.

Getting control over the spoiled brat in our head is not easy, but it's not impossible. All it takes is incredible will power and total self-control. Unfortunately, people with incredible will power and total self-control can be very annoying and not much fun at parties. Having incredible will power and total self-control can be very taxing too, because they are the kind of qualities that tend to explode and splatter on others. Have no fear. We can accomplish what we need to without them. How? We will do it with plain old consistent and reasonable effort.

## Plain Old Consistent and Reasonable Effort

Plain old consistent and reasonable effort is sort of a squishy concept that lacks the spark most people need to kick-start their efforts. When it comes to spark, most people need a firecracker in their pants. I don't recommend putting a firecracker in your pants. That won't stop some young men from doing it and putting the video on YouTube, but the rest of you should know better. Short of a firecracker in our pants, what do we need to begin this transformation? First of all, desire.

---

**Desire is an incredibly strong motivator
as evidenced by your entire life.**

---

Desire, or the lack of desire, is what got you exactly where you are today. How you spend your time, where you spend your time, what you spend your time doing—all of this is motivated by your desire. I'm not even a psychologist and I know that.

Take a look at what you're wearing, for example. If you're attired in smart, stylish clothes that fit well and flatter you, then we can all assume you have a desire to dress in smart, stylish clothes that fit well and flatter you. If you're attired in elastic band stretch poly pants and an old sweatshirt, we can assume you lack such desire and would benefit from a television makeover, even if none of your friends has told you this to your face.

By the way, it's desire, not hunger, that makes you reach for that fourth piece of pizza, which means that eventually you will have to ask yourself, what do you desire more: a healthier lifestyle or unlimited pizza slices? In fact, get to it and ask yourself that question right now. Don't answer until you've thought it all the way through. Today you may say a healthier lifestyle, but come Tuesday you'll probably be back to unlimited pizza slices. This is normal and one of the reasons old habits are so hard to break and new habits are so hard to stick to.

> **Some say it takes twenty-one days to form a new habit.**

I wish I could tell you this is true, but I have been watching my weight for decades now and I still have to think about it regularly. In other words, get in the habit of asking yourself how much you want a healthier lifestyle. You will have to answer it almost every time you see a cookie.

It's a lot like being in a relationship. In fact, maintaining a healthy lifestyle is a lot like maintaining a decent relationship. To help you see the connection better, I have created the following list of things healthy lifestyles and decent relationships have in common.

### Lisa's List of Things that Healthy Lifestyles and Decent Relationships Have in Common

1. You have to want it in the first place.
2. You have to commit.
3. You have to resist a lot of temptation.
4. Too much alcohol can lead to trouble.
5. Some days you won't care and you'll just have to struggle through it.

With a list like that, is it any wonder people have trouble with both? For what it's worth, at least as far as food is concerned, things that tempt you often look better than they taste, especially supermarket birthday cake. And if you do succumb, a healthy lifestyle is more forgiving than most partners, as evidenced by my next list.

### Lisa's List of Reasons Why a Healthy Lifestyle Is More Forgiving than Most Partners

1. A healthy lifestyle will never sit at the bar and tell strangers what a heel you are.
2. You can have a bite of the forbidden and a healthy lifestyle will not call you a cheating bastard.

3. If you really screw up your commitment to a healthy lifestyle, you can get back on track immediately without having to lie, see a therapist, or buy something very expensive to get you off the hook.

There you have it.

---

**Maintaining a healthy lifestyle is easier
than maintaining most relationships.**

---

With the desire to change your habits and the commitment to follow through, you're well on your way to success. That's all it takes: desire and commitment. Of course, as evidenced by this country's 50+ percent divorce rate, desire and commitment are easy to get, not so easy to keep up. So what else can help? That tried and true standby: positive thinking.

## Positive Thinking

Positive thinking is a very popular religion these days, especially because it doesn't require inconveniences like getting dressed up and going to church. Like most religions, it does require some small leap of faith. "Think positive," the positive thinking pundits say. "Believe and you will receive!" "If you believe it, you can achieve it!" "Basket weave? Don't sit and grieve. You can achieve. Shout 'I Believe!'" (I made up that one up all by myself.)

There are two kinds of positive thinking to distinguish between:

1. There is regular good old-fashioned optimistic positive thinking, the kind that makes people pleasant to be around, and
2. There is whacked-out sci-fi positive thinking, the kind that makes people Scientologists.

If you get confused between the two, may I suggest a reading of the timeless classic *The Little Engine That Could*? You are like the little engine. As you chug up the big mountain with your heavy load, encouraging yourself with a positive phrase like "I think I can" is an appropriate and valuable use of positive thinking. You can even make bold statements such as, "I know I can," as long as you keep chugging up the hill.

What you can't do is you can park your engine at the railroad diner, eat a big plate of meatloaf and potatoes with biscuits and gravy, drink beer and listen to the jukebox for three hours, finish up with a piece of chocolate cream pie, and then get back on the track and expect to get up the hill without blowing a piston, just because you have the right attitude.

You have to make some permanent lifestyle changes. Thinking positively about making changes without actually making any changes and expecting to see some results is, well, ridiculous, don't you think? Thinking positively about yourself, agreeing to make changes and actually making them, encouraging yourself for progress and not beating yourself up for occasional setbacks just makes more sense, doesn't it?

These aren't rhetorical questions. Don't answer before you're ready. Take all the time you need. The correct answers are at the end of the chapter.

## Affirmations

Positive thinking coaches are always encouraging their clients to employ the use of affirmations.

### Affirmations are simply the assertion of something.

"The moon is round" is an affirmation of the roundness of the moon. "The earth is flat" is an affirmation of the flatness of the earth. You can see the problem with affirmations already. Just because you repeat something over and over doesn't, in and of itself, make it true. However, if we repeat something often enough and with enough conviction, we can convince ourselves of anything. If you repeat to yourself every day, throughout the day, "I am a loving person," you will probably act more lovingly to others across the board than if you repeat to yourself every day, "Other people stink."

Affirmations, like people, come in all shapes and sizes. "I have ears like

Dumbo" is an affirmation. "I love my Dumbo ears" is a positive affirmation. "I hate my Dumbo ears. It's all people see when they look at me. No wonder I'm all alone" is a negative affirmation.

Whether you realize it or not, you already employ affirmations every day. Unfortunately, most of them are negative. This comes from your parents. In their defense, they got it from their parents, and so on, and so on. If you want to take issue with it, talk to God. He was the original bad parent. He started the whole thing when he rejected Adam and Eve and kicked them out of the Garden of Eden. Why? They disobeyed God. They ate an apple. Adam and Eve spent the rest of their lives moping around, repeating to themselves over and over, "We're bad. We're not worthy. We'll never eat fruit again." The candy bar was invented shortly after that.

# Modern Mantras

The Sanskrit word "mantra," which refers to a sacred formula that's repeated in Hindu prayer or meditation, is now often used to describe that which you say to yourself every day. "What's your mantra?" people may ask you, followed by, "What's your favorite coffee place?" Apparently the two go hand in hand, as coffee places, the likes of Starbucks, have anointed themselves the new spiritual meeting place of America.

What's your mantra? What's the thing you say to yourself over and over every day? You may think you do not have one, but I assure you, you do. Write your mantra below.

**My mantra is:** _____.

If you don't know what your current mantra is, without thinking, answer the following question as fast as you can:

What do you think of yourself?

**I think I am** _____.

I think I'm peachy most of the time, although occasionally I think I'm a rotten peach. For days when I think I'm a rotten peach, I do my darndest to change my mind.

**Life is too short to waste an entire day feeling like a rotten peach.**

How do I change my mind? I say, "I'm not a rotten peach. I'm an okay peach," a couple of times and before I know it, I'm vacuuming the living room. This is pretty much how positive affirmations and modern mantras work. They distract us while we think of something else to do.

Get yourself some of these catchy, uplifting phrases. As I said, you already have a negative one, maybe even a dozen, and it's time to beat those babies down. There's no shortage of catchy, positive affirmations available to you. I've listed some of the more popular ones below. Let's see if you can match the phrase with its source. The correct answers are at the end of the chapter.

### MANTRA MATCH GAME

1. I Think I Can, I Think I Can

2. Progress, Not Perfection

3. *I Feel Good*

4. *I Gotta New Attitude*

5. *There's No Business Like Show Business*

6. *I am Green and It'll Do Fine*

7. Make It Work

8. *I'm So Excited*

a. James Brown

b. Ethel Merman

c. Patty LaBelle

d. *The Little Engine That Could*

e. *Project Runway's* Tim Gunn

f. The Twelve Step Program

g. The Pointer Sisters

h. Kermit the Frog

## Make Up Your Own

If you're a crafty person who likes to make your own potpourri, for example, why not make up your own Positive Thinking Mantra. I made up "Basket weave? Don't sit and grieve. You can achieve. Shout 'I Believe'" in a matter of seconds.

The important thing is to come up with something that resonates with you. "I am Green and It'll Do Fine," means plenty for Kermit the Frog, but probably nothing for SpongeBob SquarePants who, if he needed such a thing, would probably be better served with something like "I'm a Square, and I Don't Care," which wouldn't be bad for Al Gore either.

Sometimes I catch myself repeating, "There are no other cases, this is the case. There are no other cases, this...is...the...case." Paul Newman said that in his academy award-nominated performance in *The Verdict*. I don't know why I like to say it, and it has no meaning for me literally, as I'm neither an attorney nor a luggage salesman, but something about it works for me. Find one that works for you.

To help you get started, simply choose one word from each list below:

| I am a | | | |
|---|---|---|---|
| | Magnet | | |
| | Joy | | |
| | Vessel | | Abundance |
| | Bundle | | Delight |
| | Big Bag | of | Wealth |
| | Winner | for | Love |
| | Nice Guy | among | Flowers |
| | Lover | filled with | Frenchmen |
| | Bucket | | Success |
| | Jar | | Good fortune |
| | Honing device | | Busy Bees |
| | Lover | | Triumph |
| | Champion | | Prosperity |

Or make up your own. Write down five positive affirmations you'd like to try.

1. _____

2. _____

3. _____

4. _____

5. _____

## To Chant or Not to Chant

For some of you, the idea of repeating a positive thinking mantra chafes deep at your core. Don't worry. You don't have to chant. I'm the first to admit that Pollyanna can get on your nerves. Besides, what would a cocktail party be without a few resident cynics? Skeptics create necessary balance. Variety is the spice of life.

Just know that the right attitude will go a long way toward helping you reach your goals, whatever they are. It makes life in general more bearable too. If nothing else, positive thinking mantras are effective tools for breaking the habit of the negative thinking mantras that may already play in our heads. Just like the teacher makes bad Sammy write, "I will not hit girls" on the chalkboard two hundred times, repetition has powerful effects. If the teacher had Sammy write, "Sammy is stupid," on the chalkboard two hundred times, one couldn't be surprised if Sammy started putting worms in the teacher's purse.

I hope with all my heart there are not teachers out there who say things like "Sammy is stupid," but one can't be sure. What is for sure is that there are parents and other beloved who say things to that effect, and not even to the effect, they say it exactly. Why anyone thinks anyone benefits from phases like "You're stupid," "You're fat," or "You'll never be anything," is beyond my comprehension, but that doesn't stop them from being said.

Unfortunately, when they're said often enough they become the mantra. If you have had to endure that kind of cruelty, I am truly sorry. And if a cupcake is going to give you some temporary comfort, go ahead and have one. But don't stay there forever. If browbeating, spirit-smashing negative phrases like those play through your head, you would indeed benefit from replacing those negative phrases with something a little more encouraging.

This is your body. You are supposed to be its friend. If you say nothing else to yourself for the rest of your life, at least, say that.

*Watch your thoughts; they become words.*
*Watch your words; they become actions.*
*Watch your actions; they become habits.*
*Watch your habits; they become character.*
*Watch your character; it becomes your destiny.*

—UNKNOWN

*Watch your food; it becomes your belly.*

—LISA PEDACE

## Tips for Using Your Catchy Positive Phrase

If you like the idea of a catchy positive phrase, here are some suggestions on how to use it:

Keep it to yourself. There are a couple of reasons for this. First, there's enough noise. Second, it's your business. Third, unless you've just caught the game-winning touchdown, going around yelling "I'm number one" is just plain obnoxious. By keeping it to yourself, you can pretty much shoot for the stars without opening the door to naysayers who like to bring everybody down.

- **Make sure your catchy phrase is in the present tense.** "I am peachy" is more powerful than "Maybe tomorrow I will buy some peaches." The idea isn't to wish for something in the future; it's to acknowledge that you are a-okay today.

- **Do something about it.** This is where a lot of people get stumped up. They'll spend a few days saying "I choose health, wealth and happiness," then they'll wait on the couch for Publishers Clearing House to show up with a big cardboard check. The purpose of a positive catchy phrase is to move you to act in a positive way today. Whether you call them mantras, affirmations, or positive catchy phrases, they are not a substitute for action. You actually have to do something.

216

- **Keep it up**. Winners never quit. Quitters never win. Spectators get splinters in their butts.

- **Feel free to change it**. If you find your catchy positive phrase isn't doing much for you, pick a new one. Try out as many as you like. They're free, like all good intentions. When you find one that puts a little kick in your step, bingo!

## To Believe or Not to Believe

Somewhere in life, we have to take a little leap of faith. Every day is not peachy. However, there are enough stinker days in any given life without us having to add to them because we aren't taking good care of ourselves, mentally or physically. What you think, how you act, how you react, what you do, what you say, what you eat, how you take care of yourself —all of that, all those habits, make up your life. Along the way, you don't have to believe in anything you don't want to. But if you aren't willing to believe in yourself, what's the point?

## Let's Sum It Up

- Paul Newman was a good actor.

- Words have tremendous power, but not quite as much as money.

- Some religions give faith a bad name.

- People in authority are often more screwed up than we are.

- Life is short. You might as well like yourself. You don't have to do it for very long.

- Thinking about doing something isn't the same thing as actually doing it.

# Reprogramming Activities

### Activity #1—Find the Silver Lining

How do you get to Carnegie Hall? Practice. Thinking positively shouldn't be as difficult as playing concert piano, but it is for some of us. I know, and I'm an optimist. So practice it, just like you'd practice anything you want to be good at. Throughout the day, force yourself to think positively. Even if you start with a negative thought, finish with a positive one. Find the silver lining.

## Activity #2-Compliment Someone

Don't just think positively about your own life. Think positively about others. Encourage people. Give out compliments. Be generous. Don't be so generous the compliment doesn't ring true. If your kid's a little slow in school, don't say, "You're a regular Einstein." He'll never believe you. Say what Mrs. Bush probably said to George W., "So what if you failed another test? You don't have to be smart to be President." (But it helps.)

Also, don't give out so many compliments people think you're trying to sell them something. And don't give the same compliment you always give. If your wife's a great cook and you tell her every day: great. When's the last time you told her she looks pretty?

Check a box for each compliment you give someone else today.

☐ Compliment #1
☐ Compliment #2
☐ Compliment #3

## Activity #3-Compliment Yourself

Throw yourself a couple bones too. Some people will find this more difficult than the last activity. If you find it difficult to give yourself compliments, it may be because you never got many compliments yourself, especially as a kid. Or maybe you just like to give yourself a hard time. Whatever the case, give yourself a few compliments today. Then check off the boxes when you do. Don't go crazy. Nobody likes a megalomaniac. The idea is to be normal, but nice. And don't give yourself the same compliment three times in a row. You deserve a little more credit than that.

☐ Compliment #1
☐ Compliment #2
☐ Compliment #3

## Activity #4—Don't Call List

I hope your life is full of people who make you feel good. If there is anyone in your life who makes you feel like crap, write his or her name here.

1. _____
2. _____
3. _____

Don't call these people anymore. Don't even think about them.

## Activity #5—Get Some Sleep

Resisting the spoiled brat in our brain is a lot harder when we're tired. That's why it behooves all of us to get enough regular sleep, which for most of us is about eight hours a night. Lest you think you're wasting precious time, understand that this is when your body does most of its repair work, like any big hotel. What's one way to increase the amount of time you sleep? Don't watch TV before you go to bed. We all know it's practically impossible to turn off *The Godfather*, even if we've seen it ten times before. Advertisers know this too. That's why they fill our favorite late night movies with infomercials promising to make our life easier. I know the advertisements are tempting. I know life is hard. Turn off your TV and go to bed. Your life will be easier if you just get some sleep.

## Activity #6—Weigh-Ins

Most people who watch their weight really do watch their weight, so get in the habit of weighing yourself. Yes, some people can do it without a scale, but if you're reading this book, let's assume you can't. Paying attention to how well your clothes fit is another way to go, but most women's clothes have a little bit of stretch in them these days. Men's clothes don't stretch quite as much as women's, which is why a lot of men belt their pants underneath their belly. In other words, you've already learned to ignore how well your clothes fit.

So, once a week, on the same day, around the same time (try in the morning, in your birthday suit for best results), weigh yourself and record your weekly progress here.

Date _____ Weight _____

Date _____ Weight _____

Date _____ Weight _____

Date _____ Weight _____

Date _____ Weight _____

Date _____ Weight _____

Date _____ Weight _____

Date _____ Weight _____

Date _____ Weight _____

Date _____ Weight _____

If you're losing between half a pound to two pounds a week, you're doing what you need to do and all you have to do is stay at it. If you aren't losing between half a pound to two pounds a week, you need to do a little more (as in eat a little less and move a little more).

*Answers to Nonrhetorical Questions on Page 210:*

Yes and yes.

*Answers to Positive Affirmations Match-Up:*

1. d;    2. f;    3. a;    4. c;    5. b;    6. h;    7. e;    8. g

Yeah, but if gluttony's a sin, I bet they have a great buffet!

# Parting Words

## Moving Forward

Congratulations. You are about to complete my non-celebrity, non-doctor, non-expert reprogramming guide. I hope it's helped. As you move forward on your own, keep in mind that life is nothing but a journey through continually changing stages. Those stages include:

- Infancy
- Childhood
- Teen years
- Young adult life
- Not-so-young adult life
- Mid-adult life
- Later mid-adult life
- Mid later mid-adult life
- Later mid later mid-adult life
- Stop pushing me
- Old age
- Underground

Wherever you are on your journey, enjoy it while you can. You'll be on to the next stage before you know it. No matter what stage you're at, remember, quality is key. Live a quality life by being in quality relationships, eating quality foods, and doing quality things for as long as you can. As you lie on your deathbed and think back on your life, watching fake reality TV with a bag of fake fat potato chips will be low on the list of things you'll miss most.

And don't forget:

**Government exists to protect business and manage people. Not the other way around.**

I know that's a hard pill to swallow. It has been throughout history. But you'll get used to it. Once you do get used to it, you can use that realization to help you make better choices. The truth is, we will always be bombarded with messages to consume more, whether it's good for us or not, whether it's good for the environment of not, whether it's cheap food, diet products, exercise contraptions, big gas-guzzling SUVs, skinny jeans, the latest hand-held electronic, etc. It's the way of the modern world. Too much industry is at stake for anyone to lighten up on the hard sell.

At least we control what we buy (both products and philosophies). I say, be skeptical. Pay attention. Ask questions. Make your own choices. Stop buying crap hook, line and sinker. Take responsibility for your well-being, and teach your children to do the same. They deserve it. And so do you.

Start now. Yes, life is a journey, but it's not as far as you think. In fact, it's more like a roller coaster. You stand in line a lot, you get about two minutes of real kicks, and then it's over. Be sure to enjoy the ride.

I suppose now is not the right time to tell you I don't know what I'm talking about. But I do the best I can. Do the best you can.

# Reprogramming Activity

## Our Final Activity—A Simple Smile Game

Here's one final reprogramming activity. It's a simple smile game my nephew, Mathias, taught me when he was about three years old. Here's how you play.

No matter what, smile first.

That's the game. It isn't actually even a game for him. He just walks in the room and smiles first. All anyone can do is smile back.

Try this for a day. No matter where you are, no matter what you're doing, no matter who you encounter, be the one to smile first.

At the end of day, you'll be infinitely lighter.

# Bib

Active Living Network. "Dr. Paul Higgins: People making a difference." http://www.activeliving.org/node/497.

Center for Science in the Public Interest. "Chain Restaurants Charged with Promoting 'X-treme Eating'" 26 February 2007. http://www.cspinet.org/new/200702233.html.

Center for Science in the Public Interest. "Food Additives ~ CSPI's Food Safety." http://www.cspinet.org/reports/chemcuisine.htm.

Centers for Disease Control and Prevention. "Obesity and Overweight." http://www.cdc.gov/nccdphp/dnpa/obesity/index.htm.

Centers for Disease Control and Prevention. "Physical Activity for Everyone: How Much Physical Activity Do Adults Need?" http://www.cdc.gov/physicalactivity/everyone/guidelines/adults.html.

*Consumer Reports*. "When Buying Organic Pays (and Doesn't)." February 2006.

http://www.consumerreports.org/cro/food/diet-nutrition/organic-products/organic-products-206/when-buying-organic-pays-and-doesnt/index.htm.

*Consumer Reports*. "When It Pays To Buy Organic." February 2006. http://www.consumerreports.org/cro/food/diet-nutrition/organic-products/organic-products-206/overview/.

ConsumerSearch. "Diet Pills: Full Report." http://www.consumersearch.com/www/health_and_fitness/diet-pills/review.html.

Cotton Incorporated. "The Fashion Spotlight Is Finally On The Plus-Size Woman." 7 July 2002. http://www.cottoninc.com/lsmarticles/?articleID=109.

Environmental Working Group. "Shopper's Guide to Pesticides." http://www.foodnews.org/methodology.php.

Federal Trade Commission. "Weight Loss Advertising: An Analysis of Current Trends." Staff Report. 19 September 2002. http://www.ftc.gov/bcp/reports/weightloss.pdf.

Federal Trade Commission, Food and Drug Administration, National Association of Attorneys General. "The Facts About Weight Loss Products and Programs." 1992. http://www.cfsan.fda.gov/~dms/wgtloss.html.

Federal Trade Commission, Food and Drug Administration, National Association of Attorneys General. "Weighing the Evidence in Diet Ads." 31 July 2007. http://www.ftc.gov/bcp/conline/pubs/health/evidence.shtm.

Food and Drug Administration. "How to Understand and Use the Nutrition Facts Label." http://www.fda.gov/Food/LabelingNutrition/ConsumerInformation/ucm078889.htm.

Food and Drug Administration. "Overview of Dietary Supplements." 7 May 2009. http://www.fda.gov/Food/DietarySupplements/ConsumerInformation/ucm110417.htm#regulate.

Food and Nutrition Service. "Pyramid Servings: How Much? How Many?" www.fns.usda.gov/tn/resources/Nibbles/pyramid_servings.pdf.

Food and Nutrition Service, U.S. Department of Agriculture. "Major Nutrients." http://www.fns.usda.gov/tn/Resources/appendd.pdf.

Goforth, Sarah. "The New American Food Pyramid." 19 June 2003. The Why Files. University of Wisconsin Board of Regents. http://whyfiles.org/179food_pyramid/2.html.

Goulart, Frances Sheridan. "Fit or Fat? Seven Sure-Fire Tests to Help Determine the State of Your Shape." *American Fitness.* FindArticles.com. Nov-Dec 1990. http://findarticles.com/p/articles/mi_m0675/is_n6_v8/ai_9223224/.

Harvard School of Public Health. "Knowledge for Healthy Eating." http://www.hsph.harvard.edu/nutritionsource/.

Kurtzweil, Paula. "FDA/CFSAN Today's Special: Nutrition Information." *FDA Consumer Magazine,* May-June 1997. http://www.cfsan.fda.gov/~dms/fdacmenu.html

Mintel. "32 Billion Plus-Size Clothing Movement Flourishes." Market Research World. 23 March 2006. http://www.marketresearchworld.net/index.php?option=content&task=view&id=573&Itemid=.

National Agricultural Library, U.S. Department of Agriculture. "Food Guide Pyramid." http://www.nal.usda.gov/fnic/Fpyr/pmap.htm.

National Center for Health Statistics, Centers for Disease Control and Prevention. "Prevalence of Overweight among Children and Adolescents: United States, 2003-2004." April 2006. http://www.cdc.gov/nchs/products/pubs/pubd/hestats/overweight/overwght_child_03.htm

National Center for Health Statistics, Centers for Disease Control and Prevention. "Prevalence of Overweight among Adults: United States, 2003-2004." April 2006. http://www.cdc.gov/nchs/products/pubs/pubd/hestats/overweight/overwght_adult_03.htm

National Center for Health Statistics, Centers for Disease Control and Prevention. "Americans Slightly Taller, Much Heavier Than Four Decades Ago." 27 October 2004. http://www.cdc.gov/nchs/pressroom/04news/americans.htm.

National Coalition on Health Care. "Health Insurance Costs." http://www.nchc.org/facts/cost.shtml.

National Heart, Lung and Blood Institute, National Institutes of Health. "Clinical Guidelines on the Identification, Evaluation, and Treatment of Overweight and Obesity in Adults: The Evidence Report." November 1998. http://www.nhlbi.nih.gov/guidelines/obesity/ob_gdlns.pdf.

National Heart, Lung and Blood Institute, National Institutes of Health. "What is Energy Balance?" http://www.nhlbi.nih.gov/health/public/heart/obesity/wecan/learn-it/.

National Institute of Diabetes and Digestive and Kidney Diseases. "Statistics Related to Overweight and Obesity." May 2007. http://win.niddk.nih.gov/statistics/index.htm.

National Library of Medicine, National Institutes of Health. "MedlinePlus Medical Encyclopedia: Calculating body frame size." http://www.nlm.nih.gov/medlineplus/ency/imagepages/17182.htm.

Nielsen. "Tops in 2008: Top Advertisers, Most Popular Commercials." 15 December 2008. http://blog.nielsen.com/nielsenwire/consumer/tops-in-2008-top-advertisers-most-popular-commercials/.

NutritionData. "Nutrition Facts, Calories in Food, Labels, Nutritional Information and Analysis." http://www.nutritiondata.com/.

Physicians Committee for Responsible Medicine. "The Origin of U.S. Dietary Guidelines." 1997. http://www.pcrm.org/magazine/GM97Autumn/GM97Autumn2.html.

PRWeb. "U.S. Weight Loss Market To Reach $58 Billion in 2007." 19 April 2007. http://www.prwebdirect.com/releases/2007/4/prweb520127.htm.

Sierra Club. "How Green Is My Workout?" http://www.sierraclub.org/howgreen/workout/?s=a).

U.S. Department of Agriculture. "MyPyramid.gov - United States Department of Agriculture." http://www.mypyramid.gov/mypyramid/adjust.html.

U.S. Department of Health and Human Services, U.S. Department of Agriculture. "Dietary Guidelines for Americans, 2005." http://www.health.gov/dietaryguidelines/dga2005/document/default.htm.

UC Newsroom. "Panel Doubles Recommended Amount of Daily Exercise." University of California, 05 September 2002. http://www.universityofcalifornia.edu/news/article/4697.

University of California, Berkeley Wellness Letter, Editorial Board. *Wellness Made Easy 365 Tips for Better Health*. Berkeley: University of California, Berkeley, 1999.

Washington University School of Medicine. "Body Shape and Heart Disease Risk: Apple Or Pear Shape Is Not Main Culprit To Heart Woes—It's Liver Fat." *ScienceDaily*, 08 December 2008. http://www.sciencedaily.com/releases/2008/12/081204133600.htm.

Weight-Control Information Network, National Institute of Diabetes and Digestive and Kidney Diseases. "Weight and Waist Measurement: Tools for Adults." November 2008. http://win.niddk.nih.gov/publications/tools.htm#circumf.

Weight-Control Information Network, National Institute of Diabetes and Digestive and Kidney Diseases. "Weight Cycling." May 2008. http://win.niddk.nih.gov/publications/cycling.htm.

World Health Organization. "Diet." http://www.who.int/dietphysicalactivity/diet/en/index.html.